Advanced Praise for *The*

"In an age crying out for wise judgment ...., ... *Leadership Killer* is an essential read. Making a convincing case for the lost art of humility, Bill Treasurer and John Havlik empower both aspiring and experienced leaders to ask questions, to take risks, to try new approaches, to fail — and to get up and try again. I recommend this book to all those who look at the state of leadership today and ask, "How can we do better?""
—E. Gordon Gee, President, West Virginia University

"With plenty of books written already on how to succeed as a leader, Bill Treasurer and John Havlik offer us something new and greatly needed – practical wisdom on how to survive leadership success. This must-read gives leaders at all levels the tools to recognize hubris in ourselves and others and develop self-awareness before it's too late."

—John R. Ryan, President and CEO, Center for Creative Leadership, Vice Admiral, United States Navy (Retired)

"In a world where leadership seems to be about who is the loudest and most outlandish, Bill Treasurer and John Havlik's new book, *The Leadership Killer,* reminds us that humility and integrity still is, and always will be, what matters most. This book is timely for those who care about leadership authenticity, and raising everyone's game."

—Mark Divine is a retired SEAL Commander, founder and CEO of SEALFIT, Inc., and Unbeatable, LLC, and the NYT bestselling author of *The Way of the SEAL* and *Unbeatable Mind.*

"You can fill a bookshelf with superb books on leadership and apply all the lessons you learn from reading them. But you'll miss a key factor. Good leaders are humble. They ask questions; they listen to advice; they admit when they make mistakes. Leadership guru Bill Treasurer and former Navy SEAL CAPT John Havlik's book *The Leadership Killer* is short, entertaining, and an invaluable resource for leaders and wanna-be leaders. You'll laugh at their stories, be moved by the experiences they describe, and, most importantly, you will learn how to be humble and how to succeed as a leader."

—Ambassador Kristie Kenney (Retired), former US Ambassador to Thailand, the Philippines and Ecuador

"Leadership is a tough job—one that requires the skillful balancing of several behavioral traits—often to the backdrop of scant information and significant uncertainty. A leader needs to be decisive, yet contemplative; willful, yet considerate; confident, yet humble. It can be a tough balance to manage throughout one's career—and yet the best leaders somehow do, without falling prey to hubris along the way. Bill Treasurer and John Havlik examine the causes and effects of hubris in the leadership mix and help us crack the code to avoid that landmine along our own journeys down the leadership trail. This book is a useful tool in every leader's kitbag."

—Randy Hetrick, Former Navy SEAL, Founder/CEO, TRX

"Leaders: I encourage you to read *The Leadership Killer* today! It is full of spot-on, ready-to-deploy wisdom that will make you a stronger and more humble leader."

—Marshall Goldsmith - *Thinkers 50* #1 Executive Coach and only two-time #1 Leadership Thinker in the world.

"A pattern seen in leaders who succeed again and again is a deep sense of humility. This quality enables them to build strong teams and continually adapt. *The Leadership Killer* offers an essential guide for readers to cultivate and leverage humility to succeed and sustain success over time."

—Sanyin Siang, Author of *The Launch Book*, and Executive Director of Fuqua/Coach K Center on Leadership & Ethics at Duke University

"The best leaders know that humility and approachability are as important as balance sheets and strategic planning. Maybe more so. Bill Treasurer and John Havlik provide a valuable resource on what every leader should know, embrace, and practice if they want to be successful in the most meaningful way."

—Tony Bingham, President and CEO,
the Association for Talent Development

"*The Leadership Killer* casts a fresh, contemporary eye on an age-old and almost universal native human tendency first articulated millennia ago by Sophocles and other practitioners of Greek drama. It is the temptation of hubris—ego, pride, the subversion of ennobling leadership into opportunity for self-gratification and reward. How could *The Leadership Killer* be any more timely than it is in these days of unfettered egotism and runaway self-aggrandizement? See the news headlines and it's clear that every leader, or aspirer to leadership, should read this well-written book with a mirror in hand, to help combat their own unjustified entitlement."

—Whitney Johnson, Bestselling author *Build An A Team*, and
Thinkers50 Leading Management Thinker

"There are two really "hard to answer questions" about leadership. The first is, "With all the money and time being spent on leadership development, why don't we have better leaders?" The second question comes less frequently, but is even more difficult. "Why do we have so many leaders who attain high positions and then fail?" This book insightfully addresses the more puzzling question. It contains a relevant and timely message for every leader to reflect upon, namely "Have I succumbed to the demon of arrogance?" Fortunately, it also provides practical steps to help all those who lead to move away from hubris and toward humility."

—Jack Zenger and Joe Folkman, co-founders of Zenger-Folkman and
co-authors of the best-selling *Extraordinary Leader.*

"*The Leadership Killer* will do more than help you become a better leader, it will help you avoid becoming a bad one! It's about staying successful in your leadership role, when temptations mount to compromise your leadership integrity. The practical take-aways will serve as a well-functioning alarm bell for avoiding the most lethal leadership pitfalls. Read this book and ensure that your leadership foundations are rock solid...and stay that way!"

—Jean-Luc Koch, CEO of Microporous LLC,
a global leader in battery separator technologies.

"*The Leadership Killer* is an uncannily timely book about a regrettably timeless problem. The disease of hubris has been killing leaders—and innocent bystanders—forever. But the infection, it seems, has spread, and Bill Treasurer and John Havlik thankfully remind us that it's time for a mass inoculation of the only known antidote: humility. *The Leadership Killer* is both a disturbing book and a comforting one. It's unsettling to be reminded of the ruinous costs of excessive pride and self-confidence, yet it's also reassuring to be reminded that there is a cure. The stories and examples are humbling reminders of how easy it is to fall prey to the disease, and the prescriptions they offer in the form of coaching tips are simple things we can each do to stay healthy and humble. *The Leadership Killer* is an important book for this moment in history, and it should be read by every leader who wishes not only to achieve success but also to sustain it over time."

—Jim Kouzes, coauthor of *The Leadership Challenge*, and
the Dean's Executive Fellow of Leadership, Leavey
School of Business, Santa Clara University

"If you are embarking on a journey to leadership, you must read this book. Even the best leaders succumb to the trappings of power, thinking their way is the best and only way. This arrogance kills curiosity, the most critical tool you will need to use as you face an unpredictable future with rapid change. Keep this book by your side for the tips and wisdom you need to do to succeed."

—Dr. Marcia Reynolds, author of *The Discomfort Zone: How Leaders Turn Difficult Conversations into Breakthroughs*

"Bill Treasurer and Captain John Havlik pack great wisdom into this short but powerful book. *The Leadership Killer* serves as an invitation to leadership that is selfless. Put down your ego, pick up this book, and start your leadership journey today."

—Skip Prichard, CEO of OCLC, Inc., Leadership Blogger & WSJ Bestselling Author of *The Book of Mistakes: 9 Secrets to Creating a Successful Future*

"*The Leadership Killer* is the literary equivalent of a super tough workout or a day of SEAL training. It forces you to re-examine your 'why' and push past your limits. Bill Treasurer and Coach Havlik wrote a book every leader must read."

—Rear Admiral Kerry Metz, USN (Retired), Former SEAL and first Commander of Special Operations Command North.

"In their book, *The Leadership Killer* co-authors Bill Treasurer and John Havlik have hit a home run. With wonderful stories and outstanding examples the authors share what not to do in leadership roles. The book also finishes with ten excellent ideas to overcome hubris and be a consistent effective leader. Great read to learn to lead yourself and others."

—Coach Jim Johnson leadership speaker and author

"In an age of arrogance and leadership gone astray, it's easy to point to ego as a negative influencer in decision making. Great leaders do lots of things right, but the underlying common denominator for all great leaders is humility. Humility is something that doesn't come easy to most. Humility is tied directly to a strong EQ (emotional intelligence). It's a hard thing to teach and Bill Treasurer and John Havlik have mastered this in *The Leadership Killer*. No one wants to work for an ego maniac.....jump inside this book and start your journey!"

—Ken Falke, Philanthropist and Bestselling Author of *Struggle Well, Thriving in the Aftermath of Trauma*

"This book is way overdue! You might think you're a great leader, but there is one lethal vice (the "Killer") that, left unchecked, can undermine all your success. *The Leadership Killer* is a must-read that when shared with your team, will prevent a lot of heartache and that makes a great gift for people who are unaware of their true impact."

—Jesse Stoner, founder Seapoint Center for Collaborative Leadership, and coauthor *Full Steam Ahead! Unleash the Power of Vision.*

"Hubris kills leaders, this is a key lesson from this book. While this lesson is one we already know, far too few of us remember it or we wouldn't so many personal experiences with bad bosses, or movies titled Horrible Bosses. This book reminds us, but more importantly challenges us to something better and gives us action steps to become better leaders and human beings. If you read this book you will be challenged to reflect and urged to action. I'm not sure we can ask for more than that from any book."

—Kevin Eikenberry, author of *Remarkable Leadership* and co-author of *From Bud to Boss* and *The Long-Distance Leader* , and Chief Potential Officer of The Kevin Eikenberry Group

"Filled with examples of the seductive nature of leadership, authors, Bill Treasurer and John Havlik show us why it's so easy to be sucked into believing leadership equates to superiority. The examples define how arrogance may be masquerading as confidence and that the only real cure for hubris is humility. This is a book that needed to be written—for the events of today and the leaders of tomorrow. Read this book. Don't jeopardize your career, integrity, and reputation. It is surely a wakeup call for all of us. The 10 Tips for Thriving Leadership should be hung on every leader's wall."

—Elaine Biech, Author #1 Bestseller *The Washington Post, The Art and Science of Training*

"Bill Treasurer and John Havlik have lived and led through challenges - as leaders in their families, in the military and in business. They write with an honest, experience-based sharing of the real trials that all leaders will face. What is power for? What gives you legitimacy as a leader? The worst use of power is to not use it. We need leaders who have strong internal compass that guides both their exercise of power, and where they choose to put limits on their own power. This book will help you develop that inner compass."

—Conor Neill, President of Vistage in Spain and Professor of Leadership Communication at IESE Business School

"We are living in a time where leadership is being discussed, challenged and debated like never before. I always tell my kids that leaders don't follow—true leaders are the ones who create the way. Genuine and effective leaders can only set ethical standards and demonstrate integrity if they are humble and release all arrogant attitudes. Bill Treasurer and John Havlik have lived careers embodied by humility, discipline and determination, and because of that, you should listen closely to what they have to say."

—Kyra Phillips, Investigative Correspondent, ABC NEWS

THE
LEADERSHIP
KILLER

THE

LEADERSHIP

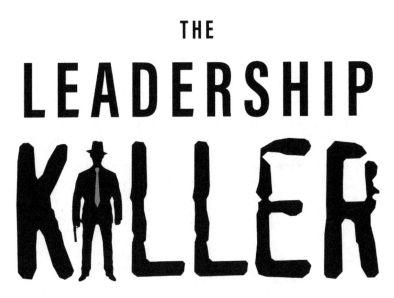

KILLER

Reclaiming Humility in an Age of Arrogance

BILL TREASURER
AUTHOR OF *LEADERS OPEN DOORS*

CAPTAIN JOHN R. HAVLIK
US NAVY SEAL (RETIRED)

LITTLE LEAPS
PRESS

Little Leaps Press, Inc.
2 Lynwood Road
Asheville, NC 28804

Bulk Order Sales: Special discounts may be available for large quantity sales. For details, call: 800-867-7239.

Title: The Leadership Killer:
Reclaiming Humility in an Age of Arrogance

Authors: Bill Treasurer
and Captain John R. Havlik, US Navy SEAL (Retired)

Publication Date: October 30, 2018

Publisher: Little Leaps Press, Inc.

Book producer and cover designer: The Book Designers

Published in the United States of America
by Little Leaps Press, Inc.

LITTLE LEAPS
—— PRESS ——

First Edition
ISBN: 978-1-948058-13-1
ISBN: 978-1-948058-14-8

Library of Congress Control Number: 2018955687

To all the leaders who humbly strive to do and be better each day.
May you hold fast to the source of all great leadership: integrity.

BILL TREASURER

To my parents John and Mary, both military veterans who taught me that
the best way to be successful in life is through honest, hard work.

CAPTAIN JOHN R. HAVLIK, US NAVY SEAL (RETIRED)

CONTENTS

PREFACE

his book was born out of frustration. Both of us are passionate about leadership, and the topic was at the heart of our rekindled relationship. "Us" is Bill Treasurer and John "Coach" Havlik. The two of us are old friends and Mountaineers. Not the kind of mountaineers who climb snowcapped summits or who forage through the hills hunting vermin, but the kind who graduated from West Virginia University. Back in our glory days, we were teammates on WVU's Swimming and Diving Team. We reconnected when the university decided to honor the 1980 undefeated team, of which John was a tri-captain. We hadn't seen each other in over three decades.

In the time since retiring our Speedos, we had taken dramatically different paths. John became an assistant swim coach at WVU, then at the University of South Carolina, and then at the U.S. Naval Academy. Captain Havlik later became a Navy SEAL officer, and served on various SEAL teams, including the elite Naval Special Warfare Development Group. In the course of his thirty-one-year career, John did numerous tours, named and classified, in the U.S. and overseas, and was the senior SEAL officer overseeing the complete redeployment of all Special Operations personnel and equipment during the drawdown from the Iraq war in 2011. During his career, he served with military leaders of all ranks, including four-star admirals and generals.

After college, Bill traveled around the world as a member of the U.S. High Diving Team, leading troupes of athletes in aquatic entertainment productions. Every day, Bill and his high-flying teammates would climb a 100-foot ladder and dive into a tiny pool below. As the captain of the team, he developed an interest in leadership, put himself through graduate school, and decided to take a more conventional corporate route, working for two small leadership and teambuilding companies before becoming an executive in the change management and human performance practice of Accenture, one of the world's largest consulting firms. He became Accenture's first full-time executive coach, working with senior executives to help them actualize their leadership potential. He launched his courage-building company, Giant Leap Consulting, after the tragedies of 9/11, and has worked with thousands of emerging and experienced leaders since.

Despite our vastly different journeys, through experience, we have drawn similar conclusions about leadership. We both know that leadership moves the world. Or rather, worlds. In small venues or big ones, when leadership is active, prevalent, and shared, results happen. We have seen leaders make profound and enduring positive changes at the personal and organizational level. But, with more and more frequency, we have also seen leaders do breathtakingly stupid, self-serving, and unethical things. We're sure you have seen these things too.

After the reunion, we began communicating more regularly, and eventually started working together, collaborating on some of Giant Leap Consulting's leadership training programs. As we talked and texted together, we found ourselves sharing disappointing leadership stories too frequently. Every few days there would be another media story about another corporate, military, or political leader who would put their entire career and reputation at stake by doing something shockingly self-sabotaging and unleaderlike. Each story caused us to become more frustrated, to the point we started asking ourselves, "What the hell is going on? Why do so many seemingly good leaders go bad?"

This book was born of our musings on that question, and our attempts to answer it. We believe that there is one profoundly lethal vice that causes leaders to compromise their integrity, subvert their own effectiveness, and misuse their power. Left unaddressed, it can cause leaders to unwittingly bring about their own ruin. This dangerously potent and all-too-human failing has formed the basis for the misuse of leadership power throughout the ages. History is littered with leaders who have succumbed to this weakness in all fields and professions. It has destroyed the careers and reputations of kings, CEOs, politicians, soldiers, movie moguls, scientists, professors, and religious leaders. This book aims to keep it from destroying you.

"It" is *hubris* and it is the single most lethal leadership *Killer*.

Hubris damages both the leader and those being led, and is the prime instigator of other subversive leadership behaviors that stunt progress. When a leader is intimidating, pigheaded, close-minded, elitist, overly sensitive to criticism, and self-preoccupied, hubris is doing its damage. When a leader is full of hubris, the most basic aim of leadership – to improve the lives of those being led – gets twisted. Hubris turns a leader's attention away from enriching the lives of others, to enriching himself.

The two of us contributed equally to this book. As the author of numerous leadership books, Bill did the bulk of the writing, but the thoughts, ideas, and tips were jointly developed by both Bill and John. Chapter 1 clarifies the dangers of hubristic leadership, and shows how leaders today are being compromised by this very ancient leadership danger. Chapter 2 highlights the universal internal struggle that all leaders contend with, and how effectively leading others starts with effectively leading yourself. Chapter 3 illustrates how the *Killer* hides out in the normal routines of your work life, waiting to strike when you aren't looking. Chapter 4 shows how the *Killer* takes advantage of your successes, to convince you that you matter more than you actually do. Chapters 5 and 6 were jointly written and draw personal leadership insights from a slice of humble pie that John was served in the SEALs. Chapter 7 ties it all together, showing you how to keep the Killer at bay by fostering Thriving Leadership – leadership that is vibrant and full of life. To close the book, we've included a "Bonus Section" with 10 specific and essential tips for being a great leader.

You probably picked up this book because you wanted practical tips to be a better leader. When we set out to write the book, above all, we wanted to make sure that the book is actually *useful.* Thus, in addition to the tips within each chapter, and the tips in the final section of the book, each chapter closes with a specific ready-to-deploy "Coach's Tip" written by John. Most SEALs are given shorthand nicknames, and throughout the SEAL community, John is respectfully known as "Coach."

In these pages, we'll share stories and insights drawn from our corporate and military experiences. Each of us has been fortunate to have worked for, been led by, or befriended leaders of influence. Our research for this book involved us reconnecting with many leaders we admire, and conversing about leadership and the severely detrimental impacts of hubris. These conversations informed our thinking, rekindled our faith in good leadership, and, we hope, enriched the value of the book.

As coauthors, each time we learn about another compromised or unethical leader, we grow more and more frustrated. Each day seems to bring example after example of leaders who have become bad examples. But neither of us are malcontents. We're competitors. Our swimming and diving days taught us that a worthy opponent can inspire the greatest performance. Our aim in writing *The Leadership Killer* is to equip you with the knowledge and tools to neutralize the deadly effects of hubris so you can recognize it, then take the necessary steps to direct your leadership influence toward noble, ethical, and worthy aims. When you fortify your integrity, your leadership will be stronger, more enjoyable and impactful, and more fully alive.

INTRODUCTION

Ego and the Harvest of Misdirected Power

Power is a powerful thing. Leadership, to be effective, involves wielding power to produce desired results. Leaders are set apart from the people they are responsible for leading precisely because of the power inherent in leading. Leaders are expected to assert power to affect results, and their effectiveness is judged by those results. The more substantial those results are judged to be, the more powerful leaders become...and the more susceptible they become to the trappings of power. It is sadly common for leaders to become intoxicated by power, more obsessed with gaining it than putting it to good use for the followers they are privileged to lead. When leaders become drunk with power, hubris is sure to follow, and followers are sure to be misled.

Leadership, ideally, involves using and distributing power in a way that best serves the interests of those being led. Hubris, conversely, upends the central service-focus of leadership, applying power not for the good of others, but for the aggrandizement, gratification, and protection of the leader's own interests. As the purest form of selfishness, hubris uses power to serve itself. It takes a tremendous amount of self-governance and discipline for a leader to direct power toward noble aims, without becoming compromised by it. Left unchecked, the acquisition of power becomes fused with a strong fear of losing it, causing the leader's motivations and actions to be directed by fear, paranoia, and distrust. Even leaders who start out with noble intentions can become inebriated with power and corrupted by hubris. The evil Emperor Palpatine, Darth Vader's master and mentor in the Star Wars movies, was right when he said, "All those who gain power are afraid to lose it. Even the Jedi."

Given that the exercise of power is central to leadership, combined with the tremendous amount of self-discipline it takes to withstand power's addictive and hubris-fortifying properties, every leader must answer a critical question: *How will I use my leadership power?*

THIS BOOK IS ABOUT USING YOUR POWER TO BENEFIT OTHERS

This book is for the aspiring, emerging, and experienced leader, and aims to ensure that he or she uses his power in a way that provides the maximum benefit to the people they are charged with leading. It aims to heighten a leader's sense of personal responsibility for leading in a way that dignifies the role of leader, causing others to seek out leadership positions and inspiring them to lead in a dignified way too. The book can provide a check on a leader's power (and ego), so he can resist the temptations and trappings that inevitably accompany being in a leadership role. The book aims to convince leaders that the privileges that accompany being a leader are of no importance when compared to the privilege that leadership *is*. Ultimately, this book is about reclaiming the role of "leader" as a noble, principled, and essential human responsibility. Now more than ever, the world needs good and ethical leaders who put their power to work on our behalf...and not for the gratification of their own egos!

EVERY LEADER MUST ANSWER THIS CRITICAL QUESTION: HOW WILL I USE MY LEADERSHIP POWER?

The main argument of the book is that when a leader goes off course, it is usually the leader's own fault. Leadership requires the mature use of power, which in turn requires focus, discipline, good judgement, and a high degree of self-management and regulation. Leaders need to continuously be vigilant to ensure that they are using their power morally, maturely, and for the good of others. Good leaders go bad when they don't do these things.

SO WHAT IS THE LEADERSHIP KILLER?

Much of this book centers on hubris as the deadliest leadership vice, a *"Killer"* of effectiveness and the clearest expression of the misuse of power. When your leadership becomes compromised by the *Killer*, neither you nor the people you are leading will be safe. Once you become a leader, the *Killer* will be fixing its tactical sights on you, aiming to take out you and everyone you're leading. Left unaddressed, the *Killer* will undermine your leadership impact, amplify the worst parts of your nature, lavishly feed your ego, and eventually cause you to mistreat others. Unless you remain vigilant and continuously develop mental, physical, and spiritual fitness, this shadowy assassin will lay wreckage to all the potential good you could have done if your leadership power had been put to good use.

There are plenty of leadership how-to books, filled with "just do this" advice. This book is more of a "don't do this" book. Learning how to become a good leader involves first learning how not to be a bad one. Of course you'll also get tips for how to neutralize the *Killer*, and, as a result, bring out the best in yourself so you can inspire the best in others. That, after all, is what leadership is all about – leaders creating leaders.

WATCH FOR SWELLING HEADS

How can you tell when a leader is becoming tainted by hubris? We like the simple explanation offered by Patrick Decker, CEO of Xylem, a multibillion-dollar water solutions company. As he was rising through the corporate ranks, Decker was fortunate to participate in a leadership development program where he received some mentoring advice from Larry Bossidy, the retired CEO of AlliedSignal (later Honeywell). Decker had asked Bossidy what to pay attention to when moving people into new and more substantial roles. Bossidy replied, "Watch for whether they *grow* or *swell*." Decker explains, "When moving a person into a leadership role, I pay attention to the behaviors that start to show up. Does the new leader sponge up as much learning from others as possible? Do they get inquisitive? Do they ask for help and guidance? Do they show humility and solicit the input of others? Do they dedicate themselves to developing their direct reports, empowering them, and creating opportunities for development? Or does their ego start to take over? Do they get territorial, focus too narrowly on their own objectives, or become jealous of their peers' successes? Do they use intimidation as a shortcut to getting people to move? *Swelling* is how you can tell when new leaders are letting power go to their heads, and the surest sign that a leader is headed for trouble."

Swelling is another word for hubris, and as Decker suggests, it progresses to other damaging behaviors. As the offspring of hubris, these behaviors work to undermine and diminish a leader's impact. Hubris is at the root of all sorts of other abhorrent and self-centered leader behavior, such as...

RIGIDITY: Backbone and resolve convey strength in a leader. But when a leader's opinions and preferences are calcified to the point that they are shut off to new ideas and contemporary approaches, their influence slowly rots. Closed-minded leadership is characterized by a my-way-or-the-highway mentality, and entire organizations have fallen because of leadership rigor mortis.

COMPLACENCY: Vibrancy as a leader depends on continuously striving to gain new skills and competencies, and embracing new approaches. Over time, though, a leader may come to rely too much on past experience, automating his response to new challenges that actually warrant novel approaches. Even a leader who starts out as part of the raucous revolution can eventually become part of the tired and entitled establishment. Complacency grows as passion diminishes. Before long complacency causes a leader to *settle*, expecting and accepting less of himself...and those being led.

INCOMPETENCE: A leader needs to have depth of knowledge to engender confidence among those he is leading – leadership competence yields follower confidence. Conversely, people will quickly lose confidence if they sense that their leader doesn't know what he's doing. Hubris deludes a leader to think he knows more than he actually does, causing him to overestimate his talents and underestimate his limitations.

INTIMIDATION: Make no mistake, fear gets results. If it didn't, it wouldn't be used by so many leaders as the primary means of motivating people. But fear has diminishing returns, eventually undermining the very returns a leader aims to get by stoking it. A leader's job should be building people's courage and confidence, not tearing them down by injecting them with fear and anxiety. Hubris sees it differently, using fear as a weapon of power to motivate and subjugate others.

INVULNERABILITY: People need to know that the person behind the leader's role is real and vulnerable, just like them. Vulnerability and authenticity help bridge the natural distance between followers and a leader. Human beings come equipped with authenticity detectors. They will be loyal and sympathetic to a leader who is conscious of his own weaknesses and limitations, and likewise will distrust a leader whose heart is impenetrable and who pretends to be invulnerable. Hubris causes a leader to falsely portray himself as invincible and superior to all others.

INGRATITUDE: Above all, a leader is charged with getting results. But results are an end, and the means to getting those results is the hard work, passion, and abiding commitment of people. A leader needs followers more than followers need the leader, because a leader's results depends on their work. It's simple really: without followers you can't be a leader. A leader who fails to express gratitude–generously and genuinely–will lose the hearts and minds of followers, and undermine results in the process. As the purest form of self-centeredness, hubris withholds gratitude because acknowledging the contribution of others takes attention and acclaim away from the leader himself.

Over the course of this book, you'll become more familiar with all the ways hubris does its damage. You'll learn from real-life examples of how this *Killer* has contributed to the downfall of many leaders. You'll also be asked to consider how hubris might already be at work through your own leadership disposition, and if so, what you can do to neutralize its effects.

It may strike you as odd that *deceit*, or some similar word, is not included in our list of hubristic behaviors. We believe that most leaders are good and decent people right from the get-go. Even though a leader who's ensnared by hubris will nearly always end up making self-centered and arrogant choices, he or she may not end up doing unethical things. There are plenty of bad but ethical leaders (though we don't think the reverse is true). There are also plenty of leaders who do bad things for reasons other than hubris (e.g., ignorance, desperation, substance abuse). That said, the leader who compromises core principles is certainly more prone to deceitful and unethical behavior, and it is these very compromises that the *Killer* wants to bring about. Why? Because each compromise removes a single brick from the larger foundation of a leader's moral structure. If the *Killer* removes enough bricks, eventually there won't be enough moral structure to support a leader's overall integrity. Ultimately, deceit, in all its forms, stems from a collapse of morality. Victory is assured, for the *Killer,* when a leader loses moral grounding.

BUT, BUT, BUT…WHAT ABOUT SO-AND-SO…?

"Wait just a minute!" you may be saying, "I know a successful leader who exhibits all the bad behaviors that hubris causes and still gets away with it!"

We hear you. Nearly all of us can point to a jackass leader who has gotten away with, and seemingly succeeds *because* of, self-centered and obnoxious behavior. The insinuation is, hey, if it works for them, why shouldn't I behave that way too?

Well, ask yourself a few questions: Do you admire the way this leader leads? Are the results this leader is getting worth the collateral damage they are simultaneously causing? Do you enjoy working for this leader? Does the leader bring out the best in you and others? After spending time with this leader, do you feel stronger, more confident, more equipped to lead? Or do you feel smaller, less confident, and more frustrated or resentful? And finally, if you could get the same or better results than the self-absorbed leader by not being a jerk, wouldn't you want to?

Yes, most of us have worked for a big-egoed narcissist and

had to tiptoe around his or her prickly personality. But just because they misuse their power doesn't mean we should. A foundational premise of this book is: **being a good leader should never require being a bad person.** Instead, we should use the leader's poor example to learn a supremely valuable lesson: how not to lead.

GOOD LEADERS HAVE PIMPLES TOO

To be clear, even good leaders have human foibles. Just because you're in a leadership role doesn't mean you should be expected to be pious, righteous, and plastically perfect. Who wants to be led by a pompous goody two-shoes? How boring!

Every leader is occasionally...

- Impatient
- Judgmental
- Intolerant
- Irritable
- Harsh
- Petty
- Selfish
- Arrogant

...in other words, HUMAN!

Even after engaging with this book and its concepts, you will still, on occasion, be some of these things (so will the authors!). Leaders are human, and human beings are a fickle and idiosyncratic bunch. This book won't ask you to stop being human. Rather, consider the book an invitation to lead virtuously, humbly, and selflessly more often.

HOW DARE *WE* TALK ABOUT GOOD LEADERSHIP?

We'd like to confess right up front that both of us have, on occasion, fallen prey to the *Killer* of hubris. We have both been the victims of our own ego-driven self-sabotage. We are seasoned but not unscathed. Many of the lessons offered in this book were earned the hard way, through our own faulty and arrogant leadership. We suspect, though, you'd rather learn from a couple of guys who have made a lot of mistakes than from some holier-than-thou preachers self-righteously pointing their fingers at you. We also believe that as you read this book, you'll draw the most benefit by reflecting on the moments when your own ego interfered with your effectiveness as a leader. Whatever bad you may have done as a leader in the past can be used as the compost upon which a good leader can grow. The whole point is to elevate your consciousness as a leader, so you are fully awake to how your own ego affects your leadership behavior, choices, and impact. So put whatever bad you've done to good use by becoming a better leader. That's what we're trying to do by writing this book.

SPEEDBUMPS ARE INEVITABLE

As you progress in your leadership career, you will face many, many challenges, obstacles, and setbacks. Be thankful for that, because facing them is how you develop and strengthen your leadership. A leader's character is defined by how he handles (or mishandles) such speedbumps. Speedbumps cause stress, and that stress can increase the temptation to misuse your leadership power. The leader who deftly manages the *Killer* will be able to learn from speedbumps without skidding off the road.

One fundamental outcome of this book is that by helping you evaluate the extent to which your own leadership might be susceptible to the influence of the hubris, and by giving you specific tools and approaches for neutralizing its impact, you will be far more prepared to deal with the inevitable speedbumps and setbacks that accompany being a leader. Leadership *is* hard, but the challenges you'll face as a leader don't require that you compromise your integrity, misuse your leadership power, or act obnoxiously and selfishly. Great leadership starts with being a good person. You'll do the most good in the world when you lead with virtue, integrity, and humility. This book aims to keep you on leadership's high road when you become tempted to take a path that's less demanding or noble. The highest goal of this book, then, is to help you put your power to good use. For others.

The *Killer* is deadly serious and means business. In the next chapter, you'll learn how even great leaders can be decimated by the *Killer*. Most leaders set out to do good. They don't start out bad. They *turn* bad, and, as you'll learn in the next chapter, the *Killer* is the culprit.

CHAPTER 1

Scary Leaders

L eadership is as ancient as humanity. Since the first tribes of barefooted humans hunted on the African plains, there have been leaders. In fact, leadership is probably older than humanity, in that animals and other organisms display leadership. Pecking orders are part of many species that have been around much longer than we have.

What usually sets a leader apart from those being led, whether in the animal kingdom or in groups of human beings, is an endowment of power. The physically, socially, intellectually, and sometimes spiritually dominant individual usually stands at the top of the heap. The earliest leaders were likely those who could climb the highest tree, hunt the biggest game, or mix the most powerful healing elixirs. More often, they were just the badass mesomorphs who could kick the asses of punier tribesmen!

Most people agree that the world would benefit by having more good leaders. We pin our hopes on good leaders because we view them as demonstrators of high ideals, people who are in some way exceptional, and who live and act with the highest integrity. But as long as there have been good leaders, there have also been leaders who compromised their integrity and turned bad. In fact, the very first story ever put to the written word, *The Epic of Gilgamesh*, centers on immoral leadership. Gilgamesh, the king of Uruk, brings us the idea of *droit de seigneur*, or "lord's right," which is the right of the leader to exercise *jus primae noctis* – the king gets to deflower the community's virgins on their wedding nights. Why? Because he can, that's why.

It's the behavioral latitude, the "because I can" freedom, that necessitates the joining of morality to leadership. Just because you *can* do things that non-leaders can't, doesn't mean you *should*. But it is also the "because I can" freedom that cause some leaders to lead in a compromised and self-serving way. The unwritten understanding that leaders and followers share is that when you're the one who set the rules, judges others' performance, and doles out the rewards, you have more unimpeded power and freedom than those who don't get to do these things. Others serve at your pleasure and are accountable to you, not the other way around.

Leadership is immensely important, particularly during times of intense challenge and change. But leadership is also massively seductive. Leaders are constantly being told how special and better they are. Think, for example, of the privileges that leaders are afforded that non-leaders don't get. Leaders get bigger office spaces (with more windows), better parking spaces, more agenda airtime, more deference, and fatter salaries. They also get less flak when they show up late for meetings, interrupt people, or skirt around policies or processes that everyone else has to follow. Even the simple fact that there are far fewer leaders than followers illustrates their comparative specialness. The fact that not everyone gets to be a leader suggests that they are cut from a different cloth, levitating above the rest of us mere mortals.

Followers build the pedestal that leaders sit on. So followers often enable embellishing the specialness of leadership. Every time followers say "yes" when thinking "no," mimic their leaders' style, or capitulate to unethical directives, they reinforce the specialness of leadership. Very often, the more special followers treat leaders, the more leaders start to believe in their own specialness. It feels good to have one's ego stroked by eager-to-please followers, and, before long, some leaders start surrounding themselves with suck-ups, "yes" men, and sycophants just to keep the pampering going.

Consider too that a huge number of organizations in the world are family-owned, including Ford Motor Company, S.C. Johnson, and Walmart, to name a few. The specialness of leadership is even more prominent when family members are appointed into leadership roles for reasons that have more to do with bloodline than competency. This is an ancient leadership game. Monarchy is leadership's original sin. It is very possible that the first ethical breach of leadership was some distant king deciding that his progeny should be the next ruler just for no other reason than being sired by the king's sperm. "I *am* special," the king declared, "and so are my offspring...forevermore!" The king gets to reign as long as his namesakes rule. It's as close to immortality as a leader can get. Long live the king!

Given how special leaders are told they are, is it really surprising that some would be seduced into thinking that they are "better" than everyone else, that they deserve more of the spoils, or that they should be free to act with impunity? Should it really catch our attention that some leaders are more concerned with the privileges that they can get by being a leader, instead of being grateful for the deep privilege it is to make a positive and lasting impact on people's lives when you're entrusted with leading them? Is it really shocking that some would succumb to thinking that they alone are the focal point of leadership and not the people they're charged with leading? There really isn't anything surprising or shocking about it. Hubris is what you get when a leader becomes spoiled.

It strikes us that more than ever the world needs good and healthy leadership, which means that the world needs good and healthy leaders. It is a basic truth that humankind's grandest achievements would never have happened without good leadership. But it is also true that the world's most wretched tragedies are always a direct result of bad and arrogant leadership. In the wrong hands, leadership, which is supposed to represent the highest human ideal, can become profanely twisted, misused, and monumentally damaging.

GIVEN HOW SPECIAL LEADERS ARE TOLD THEY ARE, IS IT REALLY SURPRIS- ING THAT SOME WOULD BE SEDUCED INTO THINKING THAT THEY ARE "BETTER" THAN EVERYONE ELSE?

LEADERS GONE WILD

Examples of leaders whose heads have been swelled by their own specialness are legion. Whole books have been written on the subject of faulty leadership. Three really good ones are *Bad Leadership*, by Barbara Kellerman, *The Allure of Toxic Leaders*, by Jean-Lipman Blumen, and our favorite, *The No Asshole Rule*, by Robert Sutton. Rather than spend the rest of this book on crappy leaders, we'll just offer a few upfront examples and sprinkle others throughout. If you want more examples, pick up your local newspaper on any given day.

- Travis Kalanick, Uber's cocky ex-CEO, displayed his oversized ego when a videotape of him arguing with an Uber driver went viral. After an avalanche of sexual harassment allegations, he was forced out. Uber was left to cleaning up the damage from the "bro culture" Kalanick created.

- John Stumpf was forced to retire as CEO of Wells Fargo after the company was found to have opened over two million credit card and deposit accounts without permission. He was perceived as blaming the malfeasance on some 5300 employees during a grilling by the Senate Banking Committee, in which one senator called him "gutless." He retired with a compensation package worth roughly $133 million.

- A month after being named "Communicator of the Year" by PR Magazine, Oscar Munoz, CEO of United Airlines, was pilloried in the press for his tone-deaf response after video emerged of a bloodied customer being forcibly removed and dragged down the aisle. Munoz initially only apologized for "having to reaccommodate" the customer, and in a subsequent message to the workforce described the customer as "disruptive and belligerent." Within one week of the event, United lost more than $540 million in market capitalization, causing Munoz to issue a more full-throated apology.

- David McClure, founder of the 500 Startups mentorship program, resigned amid lurid allegations of sexual harassment, proving that even CEOs of hipster tech companies can succumb to "because I can" behavior. After resigning, McClure posted a blog titled, *I'm a Creep. I'm Sorry.*

- Wayne Grigsby, a two-star general in charge of the Army's legendary 1st Infantry Division, was stripped of a star and forced to resign for having an inappropriate relationship with one of his female staff members, becoming the first division commander to be relieved of his duties in over forty-five years. A month later, another two-star general, Maj. Gen. Joseph Harrington, was sacked after sending racy text messages to the wife of one of his soldiers, including one in which he called her a "HOTTIE."

- Seven Navy Chief Petty Officers, the rank widely considered by most to be "the backbone of the Navy," were punished for misconduct ranging from fraternization, to adultery, to public drunkenness during their assignment to the USS HUÉ CITY (CG 66), a guided-missile cruiser.

- Robert Bentley resigned as Governor of Alabama and agreed never to seek public office again after a number of state employees claimed that they had been threatened by Bentley not to reveal an affair he eventually acknowledged having.

- Elizabeth Holmes, founder and CEO of the blood-testing startup Theranos, was charged with massive fraud when her role in covering up company inaccuracies was exposed. Her gross embellishments and deceptions played a significant hand in the eventual dissolution of the company. As a condition of her fraud settlement with the S.E.C., she is banned from serving as an officer or director for any public company. In June of 2018, a federal grand jury indicted Holmes and Ramesh Balwani, Theranos's COO, on nine counts of wire fraud and two counts of conspiracy to commit wire fraud. The F.B.I. is currently investigating other wrongdoings at Theranos, which may land her in jail.

Aside from illustrating how not to act when you're in a leadership role, there's something instructive about stories like these. They show that no matter how powerful a leader may get, or how enamored with his specialness he is, or how brown the noses of those following him, no leader gets to act abhorrently forever. No leader gets to be a god on Earth. As close as a leader may fly to the sun, his wings will melt eventually and he will freefall back down to the hard dirt floor. Call it leader karma. Groucho Marx was right, "Time wounds all heels."

LET'S TALK ABOUT SEX

There's one name you probably expected to see in the examples above, but was conspicuously left out: Harvey Weinstein.

Harvey Weinstein, as by now you likely know, was the cofounder of Miramax Films and cochairman of The Weinstein Company, the companies that produced acclaimed films such as "Pulp Fiction," "The King's Speech," "The English Patient," and many others. In 2017, numerous allegations of sexual harassment, assault, and rape exploded on the front pages across the globe. Weinstein's infamous casting couch had been an open secret in Hollywood for decades, but it wasn't until the story broke in a well-researched report in the New York Times that the story caught fire. The report, written by Jodi Kantor and Megan Twohey, led to the resignation of four members of the Weinstein Company's (all male) board. It also led to the firing of Harvey Weinstein, the dissolution of his marriage, and his subsequent arrest on rape charges. But it did more than that. After reading about the Weinstein story, and at the suggestion of a friend, the actress Alyssa Milano tweeted, "If you've been sexually harassed or assaulted write 'me too' as a reply to this tweet." Within a matter of days, the #MeToo movement had become a watershed moment where cringe-worthy stories of sexual assault that women had endured and hidden for years suddenly were now being exposed.

We were well into the writing of this book when the Weinstein story broke. Until that watershed moment, we already had plenty of examples of soured leadership, such as those listed above. In fact, we had started writing the book to make sense of all the compromised leaders we were seeing, and just maybe "be part of the solution" by helping people identify the main culprit that causes good leaders to go bad. The Weinstein story validated for us the need to write this book, and fueled our urgency to get it done.

Can there be a more heinous example of a *Killer*-directed leader than the leader who uses his power to satisfy his sexual urges? It is the ultimate act of leadership hubris. The leader who uses sex as a bargaining chip, or, as in Weinstein's case, as the tribute you must pay to step past a velvet rope, is a leader whose soul has been fully corrupted by hubris. Let's be clear, this behavior has been going on as long as there have been leaders – meaning, forever. Remember old Gilgamesh and his "lord's right"? Let's also be clear that it's not always about sex. More often it's about gratifying oneself at the expense and degradation of another. It's about control. It's about domination. It's about ego. It's about power. Indeed, short of murder, sexual assault done by leaders reflects the most egregious and profane abuse of power. The leader who believes himself to be entitled to violate the body and injure the spirit of another human being as a perk that stems from his power is spiritually bankrupt and morally dead.

In a matter of months after the Weinstein story, men of influence in every profession across the spectrum were publicly shamed, with some being forced to resign their leadership positions. Just a tiny sample of the prominent names include Al Franken (US Senator), John Conyers (US Congressman), Matt Lauer (NBC "Today Show" host), Tom Brokaw (NBC News anchor), Eric Greitens (Missouri Governor), Eric Schneiderman (NY Attorney General), Les Moonves (CEO CBS Corporation), Charlie Rose (PBS and CBS journalist and host), Morgan Spurlock (documentary director), Tavis Smiley (public television personality), Bill Cosby (legendary comedian and actor), Glenn Thrush (White House correspondent for The New York Times), Michael Oreskes (news chief for National Public Radio), Warren Moon (ex-NFL Hall of Fame quarterback), Mario Batali (celebrity chef), Steve Wynn (casino mogul), Russell Simmons (cofounder of Def Jam Records), Wayne Pacelle (CEO of the US Humane Society), Garrison Keillor (radio legend), Brett Ratner (movie director), John Lasseter (Disney and Pixar Animation chief), Jeffrey Tambor ("Transparent" actor), Dustin Hoffman (Academy Award-winning actor), Kevin Spacey (Academy Award-winning actor), Louis C.K. (comedian), Morgan Freeman (Academy Award-winning actor), and James Levine and Charles Dutoit (famed symphony conductors).

As the Weinstein story and ensuing fallout was hitting fever pitch, the story of Larry Nassar, the national team doctor of USA Gymnastics, caused a national firestorm when over 322 gymnasts came forward to reveal that they had been molested by Dr. Nassar. The abused included many Olympians, including gold medalists Aly Raisman, Gabby Douglas, McKayla Maroney, and Simone Biles. The nation was riveted as many of the women, one by one, courageously confronted Nassar in court, helping secure the 175-year sentence he eventually received (adding to the 60 years he had already gotten after pleading guilty to possession of child pornography).

As these stories came to light, we became completely disgusted, and more convinced of the need to write this book. Too many leaders we had previously admired were tearing down the reputations they had spent decades building. Too many leaders were succumbing to the trappings of power and grossly misusing and abusing their leadership. Too many good leaders were going bad.

While the need for the book took on greater urgency, the content didn't change. Hubris has always been, and will always remain, the preeminent leadership *Killer,* and, as such, must always be guarded against. What *did* change as a result of the Weinstein and Nassar stories is the book's primary audience: male leaders.

Hubris, according to Merriam-Webster, is defined as "exaggerated pride or self-confidence." Other authorities define it as *dangerous overconfidence*. In ancient Greece, the word had to do with an abuser gaining pleasure out of humiliating a victim, and included a strong sexual connotation.

Now, don't get us wrong, there are certainly plenty of examples of women leaders who have gone bad. Dilma Rousseff, Brazil's first female president, for example, was impeached and removed from office for manipulating Brazil's federal budget. Less than six months later, Park Geun-hye, South Korea's first female president, was impeached, fined $17 million, and sentenced to 32 years in prison for massive corruption involving abusing state funds and violating election laws. But because of the overwhelming imbalance between corrupted male leadership and female leadership, with men racing to the bottom much faster than women, the urgency is most pronounced with male leaders. That's not to excuse abhorrent examples of female leadership, it's just that we think this book will do the most good with men because faulty male leadership is far more common, and often more damaging, than faulty female leadership. Put it this way, if you're looking at two houses, and one of them is on fire, where will you point the firehose?

We want women leaders to read this book because, regardless of gender, the *Killer* cares only about soul corruption. That said, because of how susceptible and impressionable male leaders are to hubris, the tone of the book, and many of the stories used to illustrate the concepts, will lean towards men. As two male authors, we also feel more qualified to authentically speak to, and address, the needs and challenges of this audience. Our hope is that all readers of this book become better leaders for the people they are privileged to lead, regardless of gender.

BAD LEADERS CAN WIPE OUT ENTIRE COMPANIES

Earlier we explained how hubris can twist the intentions of even the best leaders. When a leader's thoughts and actions are directed by this *Killer*, the consequences extend far beyond self-inflicted wounds experienced by the leader. Under the influence of hubris, the wreckage that a single leader can cause can be catastrophic. It's not just a leader's reputation or career that's at risk, entire organizations and institutions have been felled by arrogant leadership. Lehman Brothers, Bear Stearns, and Enron come to mind.

There's a good chance you're reading this book because you want to be a more effective leader. You'll want to pay close attention to all the ways a leader's effectiveness gets jeopardized when the *Killer* takes over. As we have noted, bad leadership has high costs.

What Hubris Kills

MISSION: Leaders and followers are goal-focused creatures. Having a clear and compelling mission has a unifying effect, lifting people above petty self-interests. The *Killer* does the opposite. It convinces the leader that his wants and desires stand supreme. Satisfying the leader's own interests IS the mission, when hubris is winning. The actual mission gets subverted and becomes a distant priority.

MORALE: It is a leader's job to foster healthy working relationships between teammates. The leader needs to build spiritedness among the team (e.g., *esprit de corps*). When followers come to believe that they are just the machine parts a leader is using to build a monument to himself, morale plummets.

PERFORMANCE: People work good and hard for a leader they admire. The reverse is also true. Performance suffers when followers believe the leader is more hell bent on getting results or gratifying his own ego than bettering their lives.

LOYALTY: Ask yourself, who would you be more likely to give your loyalty to: a person who inspired you with courage, sought and valued your ideas, created opportunities for you to grow, and was there when you needed them, or someone who didn't? Followers are loyal to leaders who are loyal to them. The only loyalty a *Killer*-controlled leader has is to himself, severing the natural reciprocity that a nontoxic leader generates.

ETHICS: A leader is supposed to uphold and embody high ideals and worthy values. The most venerated leaders are people of good *character*, whose influence grows to the extent that they enrich the lives of *others*, elevating them to higher personal and professional standards. The *Killer* has a larger aim that goes beyond undermining a single leader's moral code. Hubris seeks to magnify and accelerate the leader's moral decay so that, through the power of role modeling, others begin to compromise their own ethics, too.

REPUTATION: As a leader, your reputation will be built on the results you get, and the people whose lives you impact during the time they're getting the results on your behalf. Leadership is always about producing benefits for, and satisfying the needs of, those being led. But the *Killer* redirects your attention away from others and on to the satisfaction of your own needs and wants. You won't go very far if the only one who thinks highly of you is you.

KILLING THE LEADER WHO MIGHT HAVE BEEN

While all of the real-time costs of hubris are high, perhaps none is as costly as the sheer loss of potential for all the good that could have been done–and all the lives the leader could have positively impacted–had he not become so enamored of his own power. The most damaging impact the *Killer* has is on a leader's potential <u>legacy</u>.

The primary job of a leader is to develop other leaders. Above all, leadership is a *tradition* that is carried and passed from generation to generation. A leader's legacy is built by nurturing and developing the talent and skills of the people who are doing the work on the leader's behalf during his tenure. At the core, a leader's most important job is not to acquire more power, but to help empower others so they, too, can find their leadership and do some good in this world, thus extending the tradition of leadership. The potential to inspire new generations of leaders gets snuffed out when the *Killer* is calling all the shots.

Thus far we've been talking about *Killer*-directed leaders who, at least on the face of it, bear no resemblance to us. But this book is about everyday leaders like you and me. As you read the next chapter, you'll be surprised to learn that there's a little *Killer* inside everyone.

TIP *COACH'S TIP*
LEARN FROM YOUR *BAD* LEADERS

Some of the best leadership lessons are gained by working for a bad leader. For example, I learned to be more decisive after working for a weak leader who couldn't make a decision. Think of a bad leader that you've personally experienced. What attributes most grated on you? What drove that leader to act the way they did? What role did the leader's ego play in their approach to leading? What impact did the leader's behavior have on you and others? What lessons did you learn about how not to lead? The best way to show that you've learned from the bad leaders you've encountered is to not act like them!

CHAPTER 2

The Killer *Within*

I t's tempting to wag a finger at bad leaders and indict them for their character defects. There's a feeling of relief in venting our anger at the misdeeds of people who so clearly assumed they were better than us. Sometimes our venting is justified. But sometimes focusing on "them" is just a cheap way to keep from focusing on ourselves. We, after all, are them.

The point of learning about the *Killer* isn't to make you better at prosecuting leaders you deem to be flawed. It is to understand how *your* leadership might be subject to hubris's influence and control so that you can prevent being subsumed by it. Everyone is susceptible to selfishness. It's counterproductive to expect your leaders, or yourself, to be vice free. Quite the opposite. Identifying, understanding, embracing, and mitigating your imperfections and vices will strengthen your leadership impact and help you lead more effectively and virtuously. There's a little *Killer* in all of us, and when you get familiar with how yours might be operating, it will have less control over you.

DEAL WITH DUALITY

Some of you may remember the old Cherokee legend about the two wolves. It's one of those folklore stories that gets embellished with each retelling, including our version. As the story goes, an old Cherokee elder is teaching his grandson about the nature of being human. He says, "Grandson, there is a great war going on inside of me. There are two wolves fighting inside my soul. One aims to please himself. He is shrewd, manipulative, and dishonest. He will climb over even his friends to get what he wants. He is thirsty for power and toxically ambitious. He assumes the worst in others and is quick to lash out in anger. His aim is to conquer, dominate, and control. He is a hungry, bad wolf that can't be trusted."

As his grandson listens intently, the elder continues, "The other wolf has a strong sense of justice and strives to do what is right and good. He is obedient in his service to others. He is disciplined and has mastery over his emotions, urges, and temptations. He brings out the best in me and others. He is a generous and good wolf, worthy of trust."

The grandfather continues, "Grandson, this war is not just going on in inside of me, but in the hearts of everyone." Then, punctuating the point, he adds, "Including your own."

The grandson, recognizing the truth of the story in himself, and eager to know the story's outcome, questions, "Grandfather, which wolf will win the war?"

Raising his hands, simultaneously pointing to his grandson's heart and head, the grandfather replies, "The one you feed."

What a wonderful story, right? It's the universal story of what it means to be a human being. Like the grandson, each of us can recognize those two wolves. Each of us has acted with virtue, nobility, and goodness. Yet each of us has acted selfishly, dishonestly, and immorally on occasion too. We *are* made up of those two wolves. Our conscience and innate sense of right and wrong helps us recognize the two wolves who live in our souls. Russian novelist and Nobel Prize winner Aleksandr Solzhenitsyn was right when he said, "The line separating good and evil passes not through states, nor through classes, nor between political parties either – but right through every human heart."

IDENTIFYING, UNDERSTANDING, EMBRACING, AND MITIGATING YOUR IMPERFECTIONS AND VICES WILL STRENGTHEN YOUR LEADERSHIP IMPACT AND HELP YOU LEAD MORE EFFECTIVELY AND VIRTUOUSLY.

THE ONE YOU FEED

At first glance, the overriding lesson from the story seems to be feed the good wolf. "Feeding" can be construed as choosing what's right over what's convenient, resisting the temptation to instantly satisfy your urges, putting your anger on a tight leash, and admitting your own contribution to situations that go south. Providing this kind of good-wolf nourishment takes intensely focusing on bettering the lives of others far more than focusing on satisfying your own ambitions. Good wolves aren't fed with lollipops and cotton candy. That's the stuff the other wolf wants.

The story also seems to suggest that you should take solace in that you are only half bad, which means you can do a lot of good. Provided, of course, that you starve the bad parts of your constitution. Interestingly, though, there is a second, less well-known version of the wolf story which suggests that both wolves can be used for good. In the second rendering, which some consider to be the authentic Cherokee version, the last line changes from "the one you feed" to "if you feed them right, they both win." Then the grandfather further explains, "If you only feed the good wolf, the bad wolf will jump more furiously to get the attention he craves. He will relentlessly fight with the good wolf and bark constantly! But if you just acknowledge him and direct his expression, he will be satisfied. Even the bad wolf has qualities the good wolf lacks, like courage, tenacity, and calculation. Both wolves need each other, and if you only feed one the other becomes hungry and unable to control. Feed them both and your inner struggle will be transformed into inner peace. When that happens you will be able to see what is right with greater clarity. How you care for the opposing forces inside your soul will determine the trajectory of your life. Rather than starve one, guide both."

WRESTLING WITH YOURSELF:
EVERY LEADER'S ETERNAL INTERNAL STRUGGLE

Contending with the dualistic nature of your own character is a central and ongoing responsibility of every leader. Unless you have mastery over the totality of your own nature, you will be prone to causing a lot of leadership damage. Gaining self-mastery over one's passions, urges, and temptations is what makes leading so challenging. This is true partly because self-mastery means going against the more craven parts of your human nature, particularly when you are emboldened with, or seduced by, leadership power. Being a good leader of others means first being a good leader of yourself, a point which we'll reinforce later. And that requires being a good caretaker for the two wolves, by giving them guidance, expression, and space. The bad wolf isn't bad if given an outlet for expression. If you enjoy fighting with people, take a jujitsu class before work each day instead of arguing with your teammates at work. Leading yourself means knowing when and how to feed *both* wolves.

THERE'S A LITTLE *KILLER* IN ALL OF US, AND WHEN YOU GET FAMILIAR WITH HOW YOURS MIGHT BE OPERATING, IT WILL HAVE LESS CONTROL OVER YOU.

Whichever story is the "real" Cherokee story is beside the point. Both versions are true in that they speak to fundamental truths. Each of us is capable of good and bad behavior. Each of us has acted selflessly and selfishly, morally and immorally. It is our dualistic inner nature that needs to be known, cared for, and managed. The first and most important challenge of leadership is the enduring struggle with the conflicted nature of ourselves. For the duration of your life, those wolves will be living inside of you, vying for your attention, wanting to express themselves, needing space and wanting to be fed. You are their caretaker. How you care for them will determine not just the kind of leader you'll be, but the kind of person as well.

ARE YOU READY TO DO THE HARD WORK?

When we asked world-renowned executive coach and author Marshall Goldsmith what makes leadership so hard, he replied, "Why is leading so hard? Why is staying in shape hard? Why is being a good person hard? It takes the courage to honestly look at ourselves in the mirror – and see ourselves the way our colleagues see us. It takes the humility to admit that we can always improve. It takes the discipline to work at self-improvement day after day. None of this is easy. Most leaders either can't or won't do it. This is why great leaders–like great people in any field–are very rare."

Leadership takes introspection and inner toil. It requires continually working on, and improving, yourself. For a combination of reasons, the more powerful you become as a leader, the more complacent you may get about doing the work. First, you're just busier and making time for self-development may seem, well, selfish when considered against more pressing priorities. Second, you start getting used to having other people do work on your behalf, yet self-work can't be delegated. Third, you've kind of gotten what you set out to get: more responsibility, more influence, and more money. The need to work harder on yourself may seem beside the point now. Why bother? In fact, though, the opposite is true. The more your leadership power grows, the more strength it will take to harness that power. The surest way to keep hubris at bay is to honor the work required to be a good leader with a continual regimen of honest self-evaluation and deliberate self-development. Mark Divine, founder of SEALFIT, says, "Humility is essential to mental and spiritual fitness, and needs to be practiced on a daily basis."

The great psychologist Carl Jung once said, "There is no coming into consciousness without pain." The work ahead will not be easy and will involve fierce honesty, self-evaluation and exploration, and, as Marshall Goldsmith and Mark Divine suggest, a strong dose of humility. The truth is, being (or becoming) a good leader takes hard work, persistent effort, and grappling with all shades of your human nature. Especially the wolf parts.

Part of being vigilant against the *Killer* is to be keenly aware of how it works against the backdrop of your everyday life. In the next chapter you'll learn how the common work pressures that all leaders contend with provide the feeding ground where hubris gets fed and nourished. Before turning to the next chapter, complete the sentence below.

On my journey to becoming a better leader and person, I commit to...

TIP COACH'S TIP
BEFRIEND YOUR WOLVES

In my 31 years in the Navy, I worked and met with many wolves; some good, some bad. Think about your two wolves. How has each wolf expressed itself in your life and career? If each wolf could talk, what would they tell you?

Give a name to each wolf. Then take out a piece of paper and draw a line down the middle. Let each column represent one of the wolves. List the *positive* attributes that each wolf has in its respective column. On a separate piece of paper, list the *negative* attributes of each wolf.

Now that you know how both wolves can serve (and deter) you and your leadership, you'll be better able to bring out the best in both wolves so they can bring out the best in you.

CHAPTER 3

Points of Pressure

L eadership is hard. All leaders will eventually confront this reality. Sure, leadership can be attractive and seductive, but that doesn't mean it's obligation free. When you're a leader, the demands on you are fast-moving and unrelenting. Your direct reports are wanting attention, fair treatment, growth opportunities, guidance, and recognition. At the same time, the people you answer to expect you to produce results. Everybody serves somebody. This is true even if you stand at the apex of the organization. In publicly held companies the CEO answers to a board and shareholders. In privately held companies the owners often answer to siblings, a spouse, and/or a board of advisors. Unless you're the top banana in a banana republic, you answer to somebody. And that somebody always wants something from you.

This chapter explores how hubris uses everyday leadership pressures as the entry point for its work. The three most common leadership pressures, and the ones we'll address in this chapter are the "Three Rs":

- The pressures associated with being **responsible** to others,
- the relentless pressure of having to produce **results**, and

- the pressures associated with constantly having to perform in the **role** of leader.

The pressure points are not extraordinary or unusual. In fact they're rather commonplace and banal. Each pressure point is universal and familiar, which is exactly why the *Killer* so easily hides behind them. Remember, hubris is stealthy. It is always preparing, behind the scenes, hidden in the ordinary landscape of your leadership life, waiting for an entry point. It is against the backdrop of the normalcy of these leadership pressures that the *Killer* can stay well hidden, ready to strike when you least expect it. For it is when you are under a tremendous amount of leadership pressure that you'll be the most vulnerable to succumbing to hubris's influence, and when you are most likely to do harm to yourself and others.

CARRY THE BURDEN OF LEADING OTHERS

Matt Walsh is the third-generation co-owner of Walsh Construction, a $6 billion family-owned construction company based in Chicago. Giant Leap Consulting has worked with Walsh for over a decade, most notably as the cofacilitators of the Walsh Group Leadership Initiative, an eighteen-month leadership program for the company's high-potential leaders. Matt and his co-CEO brother Dan have attended every leadership "summit" since the program's inception. During the very first workshop, Matt was asked *What is something about leading others that might not be obvious to young leaders?* Matt thought for a moment, and replied, "The burden of leadership." The room got quiet as he continued, "Now, don't get me wrong, leadership comes with far more rewards than burdens–like getting to develop the company's next generation of leaders. But it also comes with heavy responsibilities. In my case, as the company has grown, so too has the weight of having to continuously find new opportunities to keep everyone productively working. You're supporting families, and putting kids through college, and making car payments. Your livelihoods depend on the business being stable, profitable, and growing. I feel a tremendous responsibility to all of you. You all have given me a great life, and I see it as my job to do the same for you. And that's a burden because I am driven to not let you down, but it's also a great joy because if I get it right, I can make a positive difference in your life." Which wolf do you think he spends the most time feeding?

When you're a leader your primary responsibility is to leave people and the organization better off than when you found them. But the pressures of your other, nonwork responsibilities also vie for your attention. You're also responsible for being a good spouse, parent, son or daughter, friend, and churchgoer, for example. Sometimes it can feel like everyone and everything wants a piece of you, and that on some level you're leaving everyone a little disappointed. Oftentimes, the people nearest the leader get rooked. One prominent leader we spoke with recalled the greatest regret of his life was failing to be at his wife's bedside the evening before she died of cancer. Instead, he was on the other side of town speaking at an event. Being a good leader at work does not always equate to being an attentive spouse or parent.

WHEN YOU'RE A LEADER YOUR PRIMARY RESPONSIBILITY IS TO LEAVE PEOPLE AND THE ORGANIZATION BETTER OFF THAN WHEN YOU FOUND THEM.

Faced with mounting responsibility, many leaders push their own health to the bottom of the priority list and become self-neglectful. Workaholism is commonplace for those in leadership roles, who justify it as having a good "work ethic." Self-care becomes virtually nonexistent, and diet and exercise fall down on the priority list. According to research cited in CEO Magazine, 82% of CEOs are overweight, 69% were found to be in "hopelessly poor physical condition," and almost 60% were unable to even touch their toes!

Being a responsible, hardworking leader is a good thing, until it mutates into unhealthy self-neglect. Research also shows that 100% of CEOs suffer some form of stress ailment, most commonly backaches and headaches. Even for CEOs who are in good physical condition, the impact of sustained stress, combined with a perpetual lack of sleep, take a physical toll. Heart disease, which is hastened by stress and poor sleep, is the leading cause of death among leaders. Charlie Bell was the CEO of McDonalds when he died of a heart attack at 60 years-old. Ranjan Das was the CEO of SAP India when his heart attack hit at 42 years-old. Sam Blackman, the cofounder and CEO of Elemental Technologies, a company he was still leading after it had been sold to Amazon for nearly $300 million, died from his heart attack at 41 years-old. Both Das and Blackman had been avid marathon runners.

The *Killer* is on the lookout for the self-neglectful leader who is weighed down with the burden of responsibility. It knows that the more responsibilities the leader is carrying, the more the coiled spring of irresponsibility wants to burst forth with non-leaderlike expression. Such a leader, hubris knows, is vulnerable to making impulsive choices that give him temporary escape or relief from carrying responsibility's heavy burdens. It knows that the more exhausted a leader is, the more susceptible he'll be to character erosion, where principles can soften to the point of being compromised. The *Killer* will implore the leader to take a bigger bite of the rosy apple of responsibility, knowing that the more he takes on, the more control it will soon have over the leader.

RESULTS AND THE WEIGHTY PURSUIT OF *MORE*

To be a leader means to get results. Getting results is a fundamental leadership pressure point, and it requires keeping everyone working productively. It's a simple equation: the more productive people are, the better the results will be. And producing results, as a leader, is what you're most responsible for. Your effectiveness as a leader will be judged on the magnitude and longevity of the results you get. Period.

The pressure to get results is incessant, and the strength of the results frequently impacts a leader's mood and behavior. A leader is far more likely to be grumpy, curt, and abrasive when results are languishing than when they are flourishing. A good number of Giant Leap Consulting's clients are privately held, owner-led companies. It's almost amusing how easily you can tell the financial health of the company just by the mood of the owner. His or her disposition will be directly connected to the P&L. When profits are up, so too are the owner's spirits. When profits are down, the owner can become an irritable diva in search of a Snickers bar! The mood swings extend to the rest of the workforce. Enter the hallways of any company where people are tiptoeing around the owner, and there's a good chance that profits are down.

When you're in a leadership role, the drive for results can end up driving you. You've got to do better. You've got to produce. You've got to push others to do better and produce *more*. The engine of leadership revs to the tune of *more, more, more!* More sales, more revenue, more profit, more output, more growth. Always and forever!

Leading is more fun when results are strong and robust, so many leaders make chasing results the primary focus, the leadership *sine qua non*. The more a leader produces, the more satisfying the leadership experience is, and the more insatiable the leader's appetite grows for getting even more, *more*.

When a leader's vision becomes narrowly fixated on results, the ends can start to eclipse the means in importance, and the leader becomes prone to making decisions that are short-sighted, fear based, unethical, or just plain greedy. In 2005, Rupert Murdoch, Chairman and CEO of News Corp., the world's second largest media conglomerate, bought Myspace for $580 million. At the time it was the largest social media site in the world, and had more website traffic in the United States than Google. But not being satisfied with the company's consistent results, Murdoch and his team started to overrun the website with ads. While the move temporarily boosted ad revenue, users found the constant advertising annoying and intrusive, ultimately driving them away...straight into the arms of upstart Facebook. Six years later, Murdoch sold Myspace for $35 million, less than 10% of the original investment.

A leader can get so hell-bent on getting results that he can lose sight of the means that make the results happen: people. Results are produced by the people being led, the ones doing the actual work. When the pressure for results monopolizes a leader's attention, he becomes susceptible to treating people like expendable objects whose only purpose, he thinks, is to get results. *Who cares if people are burnt out, I'll just replace them with fresher resources. Besides, morale will go back up once we get the results we're after!*

The *Killer* wants the leader to be gluttonous for results, obsessed with getting more out of everyone and everything. If the *Killer* can get the leader to judge his worth only against his contribution to a financial end, it can make him pay less attention to all the important means to that end. The *Killer* wants the leader to intensify the pressure for results because it is the surest way to ensure the poor treatment of others. The end goal of the *Killer* is for the leader to become so fixated on getting results that he becomes blind to this fundamental truth: when you treat people poorly, you get poor results.

YOUR ROLE AND THE PRESSURE TO PRETEND

Leadership is a role, a part you play in front of many audiences. The role comes with many demands. In the classical (and stereotypical) view of leadership, you are expected to carry yourself with a commanding presence so that people know you're "in charge." You are expected to have more experience and knowledge than those you're leading, and to have timely and accurate answers to their many questions. The expectations of the role carry a more subtle expectation: invincibility. You are expected to be strong to the point of being unshakable and invulnerable. You are a direction-giver, not a help-taker. When things get dicey, you're expected to push interference out of the way and say, "I got this."

WHEN YOU TREAT PEOPLE POORLY, YOU GET POOR RESULTS.

During a conversation about the pressures of leading others, an executive vice president of an electrical company commented, "What makes leadership so hard is that everyone needs you to play a different part. Some employees respond best when you treat them as equals. But with others, if you do that you'll lose their respect. They work best following a chain of command, and they respond better when you give them explicit directives. Some want you to be an authority figure, some want you to be a coach, some want you to be a friend. And you may not even actually be any of those things, but to keep them motivated, you try to play the part they expect."

As our client suggests, the leadership role requires versatility. Sometimes the role calls for you to be tough, direct, and blatantly honest. Other times the role requires you to be compassionate, caring, and friendly. It makes no difference what your authentic disposition is; the role of leadership sometimes demands that you act against who you actually are. This is not unlike being an actor when some parts require that you "play against type."

The danger of over-attending to the *role* of leader is that you may start to lose sight of your true self. Some leaders get so wrapped up in the role that they don't know how to step out of it. They stay in a constant state of performance theatrics, pretending to be invulnerable, strong, and in control. All the while their true self goes unnourished, and, before long, they become the proverbial man in the gray flannel suit, a shell of a human being, all work and no soul. This is what the *Killer* wants. Hubris's work will be much easier if you have no sense of self, no depth and dimension, and no sense of identity beyond your leadership role. Hubris will be in a much better position to shape and define you when you have no earthly idea who you are outside of your role of leader.

YOU LIVE WITH AN EVERYDAY *KILLER*, EVERY DAY

It is against the normal backdrop of your everyday leadership experience that the *Killer* will seek its entry point. And what could be more normal to a leader than facing routine pressures of being responsible to others, having to get results, and meeting the demands of the leadership role? Pressure is mostly a good thing, and handling pressure can make a leader stronger. Pressure keeps the tires of leadership inflated; without it the leadership experience would be flat and uninspired. But past a certain threshold and over sustained durations, pressure can cause a leader's moral scaffolding to buckle.

Once your moral guard is down, the *Killer* will be in a much better position to convert your leadership from good to bad.

While hubris does its nefarious work in the banal ordinariness of a leader's roles and responsibilities, there is one leadership condition that makes its work much, much easier. In the next chapter, you'll learn why the *Killer* becomes positively giddy when a leader experiences great success. Here are some questions to consider before turning to the next chapter.

- As a leader, who are your stakeholders? Which people are reliant upon you? Who can't do a good job unless you do a good job? Who do you depend on to do your job effectively? How are your relationships with the people who have a stake in your being an effective leader? Which ones deserve more attention?

- On a scale ranging from 1 to 10, with 10 equating with "extremely neglectful," how self-neglectful are you? What is one act of self-care that you could take today? Go do it!

- How do you view your leadership "role"? Which aspects of your role require you to "play against type"? Which aspects of your role come more naturally to you?

- Describe the burdens and/or pressures you feel right now. How might they be impacting your leadership behavior? Would you say you're a good role model for handling stress? If yes, what makes you say so? If not, list some actions you could take to deal with stress more productively.

TIP COACH'S TIP
RESPECT YOURSELF WITH SELF-CARE

Exercise is a staple of being a SEAL. SEALs know that exercising keeps you not only physically fit, but mentally sharp and on top of your game. Even retired SEALs (like me) work out on a daily basis. Ask my friends what I'm like when I don't work out, and they will quickly say "moody, grumpy, and short-tempered!"

Don't forget to make time for yourself when you are a leader. Exercise, read something other than an email, find a hobby...anything that gives you a reprieve from the constant stress of being "the man" (or "lady")! No one can do the job 24/7/365, and any leader who thinks they can is delusional and a prime candidate for a lifetime membership in the *Killer's Club!*

CHAPTER 4

"Preying" for Your Success

Your loudest cheerleader during your winning moments will be the *Killer*. It relishes your successes and triumphs, and it wants you to relish them too, self-satisfied that you are the cause of all of your achievements. The world is divided into *winners* and *losers*, the *Killer* wants you to believe, and you are a *winner*. Your susceptibility to hubris's influence from common leadership pressures pales in comparison to the times when you experience rousing success. Yep, hubris wants you to win, because winning makes the ego grow. The more inflated yours becomes, the more convinced you'll become of your own uniqueness. When you bask in the singularity of your specialness, the *Killer* will be rooting raucously from the sidelines...while doing push-ups.

THE MORE YOU WIN THE MORE YOU'LL BE HUNTED

"Nothing fails like success." Words to the same effect have been attributed to luminaries that include Joseph Heller, Robin Sharma, Gerald Nachman, Richard Pascale, Allan Watts, Lincoln Steffens, Kenneth Boulding, and Arnold Toynbee. The warning is clear: be careful about getting too caught up in the pursuit of success because success breeds complacency.

It's hard to heed the warning because winning is so dang fun! Winning is the whole point of competition, the reason people work super hard and put themselves through grueling training. Winning is how you showcase your success. Winning is how you prove your worth, your dedication and sacrifice, your *superiority*. Winning a lot, though, can make you cocky.

There is a certain poetic justice in getting flattened right after ascending the throne of success. Failure seems to be nature's way of bringing humility to a fattened ego. Each of the authors of this book has experienced this personally. You'll learn about John's story in the next chapter. One of Bill's stories stems from his sophomore year in college when he won the Eastern Conference 3-Meter Diving Championship – the first diver in West Virginia University history to do so. At practice the following Monday, he strode across the pool deck like a proud peacock as he made his way over to the high board. As he thrust himself into the air, he lost his spatial awareness and started flailing his arms and legs like an upside-down stink bug. In full view of the entire swim team, the top diver in the East crashed flat on his back, practically bouncing on the surface of the water. A little humility (and a sore, red back), the universe apparently thought, will do this boy some good!

WHEN LOSERS WIN

How far would you go to win? It's a critical question each leader needs to answer. An insatiable desire to win can cause a leader to put integrity, career, and reputation at stake. When a leader's philosophy is "win at all costs," bad things are bound to happen. Consider just a few of the many examples from the world of sports.

FRED LORZ won the 1904 Olympic Marathon, for a few hours. It was soon discovered that his manager had driven him in a car for a full eleven miles during the race. The Gold Medal was subsequently given to the runner up, **THOMAS HICKS**, who had taken strychnine, which at the time was legal. He got so sick that he permanently retired from racing the day after the marathon.

SHOELESS JOE JACKSON was a beloved outfielder for the Chicago White Sox. In 1919 he set a World Series record for base hits. But his career was cut short in his prime when he became associated with the infamous "Black Sox Scandal" whereby Jackson and others were discovered to have conspired to fix the series. Despite pleas of innocence, he and seven other players were banned from baseball for life.

ROSIE RUIZ was declared the winner in the female category of the 1980 Boston Marathon, with the fastest female time in the history of the event. She was stripped of her title eight days later when it was discovered that she had jumped onto the course about a half-mile from the finish line. She was later arrested for embezzling $60000 from her employer, and arrested again for her involvement in dealing cocaine.

MARIA SHARAPOVA was a five-time top female singles tennis player in the world, an Olympic medalist, and the only Russian to have won the career Grand Slam. Yet, in 2016, the International Tennis Federation prohibited her from playing tennis for two years after she tested positive for a banned substance.

TONYA HARDING was the 1994 U.S. figure staking champion and medal contender at the 1994 Olympics. But her title was stripped and she was banned from U.S. Figure Skating Association for life after her ex-husband, Jeff Gillooly, was found guilty of orchestrating an assault on Harding's skating rival, Nancy Kerrigan. Harding got probation for conspiring to hinder the prosecution of her husband. The New York Times called the Harding/Kerrigan story "one of the biggest scandals in American sports history."

MARION JONES won five track-and-field medals at the 2000 Olympics, the first woman ever to have done so. After admitting to using banned substances, she was forced to return all her medals in 2007.

ALEX "A-ROD" RODRIGUEZ is considered one of the greatest baseball players of all time, with over 3000 hits, 2000 RBIs, and 696 home runs. But the 14-time All Star's career was tainted by steroid use, which he admitted to, explaining that he did so due to an "enormous amount pressure to perform." He was suspended from playing the entire 2014 season. A tiny sample of other star major league players to have been implicated with performance enhancing drug use include Jose Canseco, Barry Bonds, Roger Clemens, Wally Joyner, Sammy Sosa, Rafael Palmeiro, Mark McGuire, and Manny Ramirez.

LANCE ARMSTRONG won the Tour de France an extraordinary seven times...all by cheating. In 2012 he was banned from Olympic sports for life and stripped of his seven Tour de France titles after reluctantly admitting doping with illegal performance enhancing substances.

ALEXANDER KRUSHELNITSKY won the bronze medal for mixed doubles curling at the 2018 Winter Olympics, with his wife, Anastasia Bryzgalova. But they were stripped of the medal after he tested positive for using Meldonium, a banned substance. Yes, the desire to win can become so strong that cheaters can even be found in the sport of curling. Curling!

GILGAMESH LIVES!

It's striking how many leadership nosedives begin at the pinnacle of success. General David Petraeus stood on a mountain of successes before his breathtaking fall. He graduated from West Point as a distinguished cadet (top 5% of his class). He won the prestigious General George C. Marshall award as the top graduate of the U.S. Army Command and General Staff College. He earned a Master's in Public Administration and a Ph.D. in International Relations from Princeton University. He became a four-star General and oversaw all coalition forces during the Iraq war. His "surge" strategy is largely credited with turning around and helping win the Iraq war. After serving 37 honorable years in the U.S. Army, the Senate *unanimously* confirmed him to lead the CIA.

General David Petraeus was, and is, an American patriot. Entire books have been written on his astonishing and stellar career. One book, though, stands out as particularly revealing, and not because of the book's content. What makes *All In: The Education of David Petraeus* so unique is that during the book's writing, while he was the Director of the CIA, Petraeus put all of his accumulated successes and entire reputation at risk by having an affair with the book's coauthor, Paula Broadwell. A subsequent FBI investigation discovered that Petraeus and Broadwell had been exchanging romantic emails...and top-secret classified information. Acknowledging the extramarital affair, he resigned from the CIA and, eventually, pled guilty in federal court to one misdemeanor charge of mishandling classified information. But the damage to his career and, more importantly, his reputation, was lasting.

IT IS STRIKING HOW MANY LEADERSHIP NOSEDIVES BEGIN AT THE PINNACLE OF SUCCESS.

Why? Why would a leader with such a sterling reputation put everything at risk for sex? It's worth remembering the honor code that all West Point cadets live by: "A cadet will not lie, cheat, steal, or tolerate those who do." This formalized code is the *minimum* standard of ethics expected of all West Point cadets, a code so sacred that many graduates adhere to its standards well past their days at the Academy, indeed, for the duration of their lives!

There are no easy answers to why General Petraeus's compromised his reputation. Good leaders do bad things for multiple reasons, often involving one's psychological constitution, family upbringing, recent tragedy or loss, low self-esteem, for example. In the case of General Petraeus, and so many others, sometimes it's simply the overwhelming power of lust and a serious lack of groin management. General Petraeus wouldn't be the only leader willing to put everything at risk for sex. In the Bible, King David, who creepily watches Bathsheba bathe from afar, starts a torrid affair with her, and ultimately causes her husband's death. Mark Antony, the Roman general, was married when he started his sizzling affair with Cleopatra, the Egyptian ruler who bore him three children. The affair played a large part in causing a Roman civil war. They died in each other's arms after committing suicide. If history is our judge, General Petraeus, by acknowledging and ending his affair quickly, actually got off easy.

It seems that the greater the success a hubristic leader achieves, the more spectacular the fall will be. Petraeus's case is not unlike that of Elliot Spitzer, who had become Governor of New York after six highly successful years as the Empire State's Attorney General. He was Governor for less than one year when he was forced to resign after *The New York Times* reported that he had been a regular customer at a high-priced escort service called Emperor's Club VIP.

For some leaders, their own success becomes the justification for the-rules-don't-apply-to-me behavior. "Look at all that you've accomplished," the *Killer* tells them. "You deserve this pleasure! It's a small reward for all the good work you've done on behalf of others!" There's more than a hint of deficit thinking involved when a leader feels that they deserve *more*. The desire for more, whether it's sex, money, power, whatever, is often an inverse reflection of the inadequacy, the *lessness* or *not-enoughness*, the leader feels at the soul level. The bigger the soul chasm, the more voracious the appetite to fill it. A leader who portrays a deserving Big King VIP on the outside to mask deep feelings of inadequacy on the inside wants to please himself and degrade himself at the same time. He is just the kind of leader who could be expected to bed an escort at the Emperor's Club.

SUCCESS STRENGTHENS THE *KILLER*

Success makes you an easy target for the *Killer*. It wants it as badly as you do. Why? Because it's precisely when you're basking in the light of your achievements that your flanks and backside will be left unprotected. Success, by providing you with incontrovertible proof of your value, can cause you to let your guard down. It can twist your sensibilities to the point that you feel deserving of special exemptions – call it *Leadership Latitude*. The *Killer* wants you to believe that you're apart from and *above* others, and that your specialness should be rewarded with certain freedoms that lesser, non-successful people, don't get to enjoy. The more you love your success, the more you make chasing it the focal point of your leadership, the easier it will be for the *Killer* to get working inside you. Your obsession with success portends the failure that the *Killer* is working hard to bring you.

The key isn't to devalue success. The key is to not get so enamored with it that you start to compromise your integrity in pursuit of it.

THE DESIRE FOR MORE, WHETHER IT'S
SEX, MONEY, POWER, WHATEVER, IS
OFTEN AN INVERSE REFLECTION OF
THE INADEQUACY, THE *LESSNESS* OR
NOT-ENOUGHNESS, THE LEADER FEELS
AT THE SOUL-LEVEL. THE BIGGER THE
SOUL CHASM, THE MORE VORACIOUS
THE APPETITE TO FILL IT.

DO THE NEXT RIGHT THING

Success feels good, especially when it's deserved. But success in and of itself isn't the point of leadership. Success is an outcome. The point of leadership isn't some pot of gold you hope to get by being a leader. Rather, it's about the positive impact that your leadership can have on the people you're leading, and by extension the organization you're serving, by embodying a set of values and virtues as you meet challenges that push against them. Leadership, essentially, is about doing the next right thing when the temptations for doing wrong are high. Enduring leadership satisfaction comes not because of the extra freedoms you enjoy because of your accumulated successes. It comes from the lives that have been positively impacted through your integrity.

In the next chapter we'll home in on the lethality of hubris. As an added bonus, you'll learn how, for a while, hubris took one of the authors down. Before turning to the next chapter, though, and to make sure you get the most out of the chapter you just read, answer the questions below.

- Can you look in the mirror and be proud of the leader you see looking back at you?

- Think of a time when life let you know that you had gotten too cocky. What caused you to become so full of yourself? What outcome did the cockiness lead to? What did you learn about yourself in the process? How do you honor those lessons in the way you lead today?

- What leadership values do you believe yourself to embody most of the time? What specific actions could you take to embody them more fully, more often?

- What do you view as the whole point of your leadership?

- Describe one leadership "do over" you wish you could have. What do you regret about the way you contributed to the episode? What did you learn about yourself in the process? What is one action you could take to honor the lessons you learned from your "do over moment"?

- What line will you draw between an aggressive will to win and wanting to win so badly you're willing to cheat?

COACH'S TIP
PUT THE MISSION AND
TEAM ABOVE YOURSELF

One of the central lessons that a new SEAL officer must learn is that the overall team mission should always come before the individual. Additionally, you have to learn not to get so enamored by mission success that you start to compromise your (and the Navy's) core values in pursuit of it. Serving the mission with honor should be your truest aim.

Winning feels good. Wanting to win is healthy. But your desire to win should never undermine your integrity or be used as an excuse to do wrong by others. Captain Spock of the U.S.S. Enterprise said it best in Star Trek II: The Wrath of Kahn: "Logic clearly dictates that the needs of the many outweigh the needs of the few."

CHAPTER 5

All Hail Supreme General Hubris

ubris is a commanding general, the guy in charge. The more hubristic a leader is, the more wanton, unrestrained, and degenerate he will be. You see General Hubris doing his work when a leader exchanges self-restraint and humility for arrogance and self-interest. If good leadership starts with leading oneself, hubris is the best evidence that a leader is misleading himself.

The Latin word for "I" is ego. Hubris results from overindulging and feeding the ego, eroding a leader's character at a foundational level, to the point of eventual implosion. As hubris builds, character and humility slowly decay, sometimes over years or decades. Each small selfish decision, each act of ego indulgence, corrodes a leader's moral foundation until it gets so compromised, so weakened, so jaded that it buckles. A central warning across the ages, from the Bible to Shakespeare to the present day, is that the fall of one's character, and all the peripheral damage that character erosion causes, is preceded by the overinflation of pride.

As we pointed out in the first chapter, leadership is massively seductive. Leaders get special treatment, often to the point that they come to believe that they are, in fact, more than special – they are superior. It's easy to fathom how a leader might become convinced of his own superiority, given that in many organizations we still refer to our leaders as our "superiors." A high organizational rank, though, should not equate with human superiority, and self-leadership requires the leader to be conscious, self-aware, and awake to all the ways he is, in fact, not superior. He is merely assigned more power and responsibility to get results on our behalf.

BE CONFIDENT WITHOUT SLIPPING INTO OVERCONFIDENCE

When it comes to leadership, one important consideration is the kind of leader people willingly follow. Authentic leader confidence is important to followers. We want our leaders to have a backbone, genuine convictions, and a strong sense of self. We want to be led by leaders who are comfortable with who they are, and not squirrely in their skin. We want leaders who can make tough decisions without waffling. Yes, we want our leaders to be confident. But we don't want them to be overconfident. There are fewer turnoffs as damaging to group loyalty as a leader's arrogance. When confidence slips over into conceit (hubris), the focus of leadership shifts from service to self-interest. Most followers will withhold loyalty from the leader they think is strictly out for his own best interests.

Much of the focus of Bill's previous book, *A Leadership Kick in the Ass*, is on the negative consequences of leadership vanity. The title of the book is not about the butt-kicking that leaders should give others, but about the self-inflicted kicks leaders receive as a result of their own self-absorption. The book explores the critical and counter-balancing relationship between confidence and humility, and how followers want the presence and harmony of both. As the book notes, the best leaders, the ones we most want to follow, are centered, grounded, and nontoxic. They lead not so their power can grow, but so everyone else's can. Through giving the best of themselves, they draw out the best in everyone.

It is the lack of humility and genuine caring that followers find so repulsive and dangerous in arrogant leaders. Hubris causes a leader to trust and value his own judgment above all others, closing himself off from valuable feedback that could otherwise make for better decisions. Hubris is what makes a leader demand loyalty, not because it's deserved, but because it forces everyone to keep the leader at the forefront of their attention. Hubris causes a leader to become overconfident in the face of risk, presuming that his superior judgment will stack the odds in his favor. When a leader lacks humility, followers get anxious because they bear the full brunt of whatever poor decisions or miscalculated risks the arrogant leader takes. Leader overconfidence causes followers to lose confidence in the leader.

Followers value the presence of humility because it serves as an important ego-mitigating function. They will afford a leader a lot of power as long as they know that power is tethered to humility. People want to know that no matter how much success you've achieved, no matter how much influence and authority you have, you haven't forgotten your roots. They want to know that you wear right-sized britches and that you put them on the same way they do. But if a leader's ego becomes inflated and untethered from the grounding influence of humility, followers will unfollow the leader fast.

LEADER OVERCONFIDENCE CAUSES FOLLOWERS TO LOSE CONFIDENCE IN THE LEADER.

ARROGANCE MASKS AS CONFIDENCE? YEP.

The *Killer* of hubris can be surprisingly cunning and subtle, often blurring the distinction between healthy confidence and unhealthy arrogance. It's healthy, for example, for a newly minted middle manager in charge of a new team to want to show his boss that he'll work with gusto to get the job done. It's unhealthy, though, for that same manager to think he can do it all himself. Plenty of middle managers plateau because they can't shift from being a doer to being a delegator...the one who has oversight over those who are supposed to do it. They struggle making the shift from self-performing work to coaching their team's performance. They micromanage so much they might as well be doing the task themselves. Before long, they get so oversaturated doing or micromanaging tasks that they become a bottleneck for the team's progress, inhibiting performance and demoralizing the team. It's not just lack of delegation skills that causes a manager to take on too much himself, it's arrogance masked as confidence.

A similar example of how arrogance gets masked as confidence is a new leader refusing to ask for help, in an effort to show his boss that he can handle challenges without having to bother the boss. He'll say with pride, "Don't worry boss, I've got this!" Then, when complex challenges occur, rather than ask for his boss's or team's help, he'll try to deal with it himself, often delaying informing his boss until what started out as a small issue that could have been solved by simply asking for other's support, becomes a full-blown, very embarrassing, and sometimes job-ending problem.

A little humility could have prevented the mess. It was hubris, not confidence, that caused the manager to think he could solve all challenges by himself, hubris that kept him from asking for help, and hubris that caused him to wait too long to inform his boss. And while the hubris in situations like these may not rise to the level of, say, a lustful romp at The Emperor's Club, it's still hubris and even in small doses can be highly damaging.

HUBRIS GETS EVEN THE BEST OF US

In the last chapter we shared a story about how Bill's cockiness resulted in a humiliating back-smacker in front of his teammates. Now it's time for part 1 of Captain John Havlik's story.

First, some background. To become a Navy SEAL, it takes a candidate over a year from starting Basic Underwater Demolition/SEAL (BUD/S) school to graduation...if they're lucky enough to finish. BUD/S training is widely regarded as the most physically and mentally demanding training program in the entire U.S. military, with the average class attrition rate being approximately 70%. The most intense part of BUD/S is the infamous "Hell Week," where candidates will only get an estimated 4 hours of sleep *during the entire week,* with many days involving as much as 20 hours of continuous physical training of some sort. If you've got what it takes to survive Hell Week, then successfully complete the rest of BUD/S training to become a Navy SEAL, in laymen's terms, you're a stud. (Bill wrote that, not John!)

After graduating BUD/S, then Ensign John Havlik (and his growing hubris) was riding high! Like any good junior officer, John was eager to become "operational" and lead SEALs. After doing well as an Assistant Platoon Commander on two overseas deployments, he was finally awarded his own platoon, officially becoming the "Officer in Charge" of 14 SEALs. As a direct result of excelling as a Platoon Commander, John volunteered and was nominated by his SEAL Team Commanding Officer (CO) for assignment to the Naval Special Warfare Development Group (DEVGRU), the SEAL's most elite operational unit.

In addition to being nominated for DEVGRU by your CO, each SEAL volunteer must pass a stringent interview and screening process conducted by a panel of DEVGRU operators and support personnel. Then, after being selected, each selectee must successfully complete an extremely intense and high risk 6-8 month Selection and Training (S&T) Program. Like BUD/S, the S&T attrition rate is high, usually around 50%. The reason the process is so intense and selective is that DEVGRU is widely considered the very best of the best in the SEAL community, the team that performs only the most highly sensitive operations.

Now, John is old school, so there's a lot we can't tell you about his Special Ops service. Even today during Giant Leap Consulting's leadership workshops, when people ask John a question that the Navy would frown upon him answering, he simply replies, "How's the weather in Tampa?" This much we can tell you, though: as part of DEVGRU, John went from commanding a platoon of 14 SEALs to leading a team of over 40 of the very best SEAL operators. DEVGRU was fun, it was exciting, it was challenging, it was dangerous, it was KICKASS... but it was also very "political." John (and his hubris) loved everything about DEVGRU...except for the politics.

After DEVGRU, John took an overseas assignment as the Executive Officer (XO) in charge of approximately 200 military personnel. As the XO, John was the second-ranked officer in the unit, junior only to the Commanding Officer (CO), and responsible for the day-to-day operation of the command. Very few junior officers earn the chance to be assigned to such a challenging billet, and being XO of a special operations unit in a foreign country was the kind of opportunity that every junior officer yearned for. Why? Because foreign assignments are harder and full of challenges not normally associated with U.S.-based assignments, with even minor incidents having the potential to become international incidents. And, leading in a foreign country is ultimately a great way to prove to the brass that you've got what it takes to someday join their ranks.

PRIDE COMETH FOR THE SEAL

John felt extremely confident in the XO role, benefitting from all his previous SEAL training and experience. He loved leading and working with teams of committed personnel who were eager to do a good job. But the most challenging part of John's job was dealing with the "Big Navy" and its annoying politics. You see, being a SEAL is far more unconventional, improvisational and far less regimented than being part of the conventional "Big Navy." SEALs are given much greater autonomy and flexibility, and dealing with the burdensome Navy politics had always been the least enjoyable part of John's job (and career), one which he avoided as much as possible.

Because of inclement weather in Tampa, we aren't at liberty to share the full scope of his covert work, but we can tell you, though, the work was challenging, complex, and required lots of leadership from John. His confidence, and hubris, was growing. He felt sure that he'd be promoted from his current rank of Lieutenant to Lieutenant Commander. He felt certain he had dutifully checked all the promotion boxes. He had been successful in multiple operational SEAL platoon leadership roles, done well at DEVGRU, and had taken on several tough overseas leadership assignments. He was confident and ready for the additional responsibility...and the higher pay grade it came with!

SEALING FATE

John knew he was eligible for promotion when he had started his XO tour. Getting promoted in the Navy is a lengthy process, and John had been in his XO role for nearly a full year before learning the results of his first "look" for promotion to Lieutenant Commander: DENIED!!!

It was a huge and bitter blow to John's ego. He was sure that he had met all the marks. Even his CO was perplexed, telling him he thought it was "bullshit." Wanting to know what the Navy thought he had done wrong and what he could do better, John contacted the only SEAL officer on the promotion board.

But because Navy promotion board proceedings are secret, and each promotion board member takes an oath to honor that secrecy, to John's great frustration, his fellow SEAL wouldn't reveal any real reason or background on why John's promotion had been denied. "I hate Navy politics!" John thought.

Knowing he had one final promotion opportunity, John worked extremely hard to publicly stay fully motivated and engaged in his current XO assignment. Privately, though, John couldn't let the failure to promote go. The worst part was not knowing the reason for the denial. If something was broken, he needed the feedback to fix it. Instead, he wracked his brain over and over for a year, trying to figure out what he had done wrong. It's a fixation that doesn't lend itself to staying motivated, and John could feel his motivation slipping fast.

You might think that things couldn't get much worse for XO John Havlik. You'd be wrong. Despite busting his hide to make himself more "promotable" on his second look for Lieutenant Commander, a year later John was passed over for promotion *again*, and as a result, he was forced out of the two things he loved most in life...the Navy and the SEALs.

As said earlier, the *Killer* of hubris acts in subtle ways. As you read John's story, did you catch it at work? Think about it. Why would John Havlik assume that he could avoid becoming skilled at dealing with the politics of a highly political organization, and be promoted throughout his career solely on past superior performance in the right career assignments? The Navy *is* political. Presidents Kennedy, Johnson, Nixon, Ford, Carter, and George H.W. Bush all served in the Navy, just as scores of other politicians have. What's so special about John that he would get to sidestep learning how to navigate the political realities of an inherently political system? No naval officer gets special dispensation from having to deal with Navy politics, not even those with more wild and independent spirits such as the SEALs. John's contribution to his getting dismissed from the Navy SEALs was that he had let his hubris and aversion to "Navy politics" become a leadership flaw and his blind spot. The Greek origin of the word *politics* connects to the idea of using one's power for the common good of the citizenry. In the purest sense, politics has everything to do with healthy leadership. To his own misfortune, hubris tainted John's view of politics so that he saw it as bothersome, annoying, and ignoble.

Notice too how the *Killer* of hubris places John as the victim of his story. He viewed his not getting promoted as an insult being done *to* him. He saw it as injustice to which he was powerless to influence, despite excelling throughout his Navy career!

Recall, though, that this is part 1 of John's story. We'll revisit the story later when we get to the solutions part of the book. A true SEAL doesn't quit, and would never let a good failure go to waste.

SELF-LEADERSHIP PREVENTS HUBRIS

Before you can successfully lead others you've got to successfully lead yourself. Keeping one's ego in check, because of all the ways a leader's ego can grow hungry to be fed, is the most important part of self-leadership. It takes being alert to the subtle ways the *Killer* of hubris might be working in you. Are you grumpy because you're not getting something you feel you deserve? Are you playing the hero and taking on tasks you should no longer be doing? Are you above asking for help? Have you become convinced that you are the victim in your leadership story? If so, hubris may have begun to kill your leadership.

As this chapter comes to a close, we feel that it's appropriate to share a quote from our friend Vice Admiral John Ryan, U. S. Navy (retired), and current CEO and President of the Center for Creative Leadership, a renowned leadership education and development institution. He sums up the importance of being vigilant against hubris this way: "In all fields, you're graded as a leader according to two dimensions: you leading and managing you, and you leading and managing others. The first cannot be outsourced and is the hardest and most important to do as we advance in our careers. Without self-regulation, genuine humility, and learning agility, leaders will slip into hubris and excellence cannot be sustained."

BEFORE YOU CAN SUCCESSFULLY
LEAD OTHERS YOU'VE
GOT TO SUCCESSFULLY
LEAD YOURSELF.

Hubris is the greatest of all leadership temptations, and, as John Ryan suggests, it takes great inner strength and self-discipline for a leader to stay grounded in the common humanity he shares with those he is privileged to lead.

Here are some questions worth considering and actions worth taking before turning to the next chapter.

- On a scale ranging from 1 – 10, with 10 being "very confident", how confident are you in your current leadership role? What makes you justify the number you picked?

- Describe a time when you took on more than you could handle. What caused you to do that? What were the consequences? What role might hubris have played in this story?

- In your role as a leader, when was the last time you asked for help? On a scale ranging from 1 – 10, with 10 being "very easy," how easy was it for you to ask for help? If asking for help is challenging for you, what makes it challenging?

- Think of a leader you admire for his or her humility. How does humility contribute to your admiring him or her? What impact does their humility have on your view of them?

- How would your direct reports answer the last question regarding you? Do you think you're viewed as a leader who demonstrates humility? What makes you think so?

- Action: Monitor your "I" to "we" ratio. When telling a story, or sharing ideas with your team, if you use the word "I" more than the word "we," hubris is probably subverting your leadership!

TIP COACH'S TIP
BE AWARE OF YOUR BLIND SPOTS

Boy, did my hubris get me into some trouble. You'll learn more about my story in the next chapter. In the meantime, my advice to you is to start paying attention to how your ego can deflect your attention away from your leadership blind spots. Sometimes the thing you're avoiding is the very thing you need to address. I hated Navy politics and wanted nothing to do with it. So I avoided situations or people who I dismissed as political. I ignored getting a mentor (or "sea daddy" in Navy lingo), a senior officer I respected that I could call upon for career advice. I tried to go solo, and the consequence for doing it my way, and ignoring the political nature of leadership, was that I "failed to promote" and subsequently got kicked out of the Navy and the SEALs.

What blind spots might your ego be keeping you blind to? What people or situations do you consistently avoid and why? What have been the positive and negative consequences of your avoiding those situations or people?

List three actions you will commit to taking in order to confront what you've been avoiding:

1.

2.

3.

CHAPTER 6

Leadership Starts at the Bottom

Thirteen years. That's how long John Havlik had been in the Navy before they issued him his walking papers. Thirteen years of busting his hump to complete what is widely considered to be the most physically and mentally demanding training in the U.S. military, multiple overseas deployments and assignments, and living the high life of a SEAL officer.

It was all he knew, and now it was all gone.

Nothing in his SEAL experience even came close to the shock John felt after being passed over for promotion a second time – *even the time on deployment when he was shot in the arm (with a live round) by a negligent fellow SEAL* during a training event. With nowhere to go, he went home to live with his parents...at 37-years old. Thank God they still had a bed for him – the one he hadn't slept in since he went off to college some 20 years earlier.

All his life John had strived to reach for the hardest goals, the goals many of his friends, and all of his detractors, said he couldn't/wouldn't achieve. As a Hall of Fame swimmer in college, showing up for countless hours and miles of double practices each day, all for the sole purpose of swimming faster than everybody else, gave him purpose and direction. Later, becoming an elite Navy SEAL helped separate and distinguish him from others. But now he felt lost at sea, rudderless, with no plan. He had no mooring. He had no challenges. He had no purpose. And back living in his parent's house, he had absolutely no life.

When low can't go lower, eventually you hit a bottom, and bottoms, personally and professionally, are profoundly important. Everything gets rearranged at the bottom: your hopes, your dreams, your memories, and most importantly, your ego. As lonely as the bottom is, you are not alone. You are with your two wolves. In the depths of the bottom, your truest nature, with all its complexities and contradictions, is revealed and you are left to grapple with yourself. It's at this absolute bottom where you learn who you really are, and what you're truly made of.

There's something else that can happen at the bottom, if you let it. It humbles you. The bottom is where hubris weakens. If you allow yourself to endure the hard bedrock of the bottom, and if you open yourself up to the lessons it can teach you, the bottom will eventually reveal your next right action. The bottom wants you to know your truest truth. At John's bottom one thing had become crystal clear: down deep in his core, John knew he was a SEAL and SEALs don't quit. He had something to prove after all.

John had a new goal: get back in the Navy and serve his country…no matter what it took, no matter how long it took, John was determined to get back on active duty and be a SEAL again.

DON'T QUIT

John *LOVES* to work out. As he puts it, working out keeps him sane. A grueling workout, whether in the pool or gym, is where John does his best thinking. Once he resolved to get back in the Navy, he knew he had to stop feeling sorry for himself, get his lazy ass off the couch, and start working out like a fanatic again, which he did. He knew he'd have be in tip-top shape, mentally and physically, to have even a fighting chance to get back in the Navy. He also knew that his parent's house was no place to start a comeback. So he reached out to a good college buddy who was living in Knoxville, Tennessee, who generously offered John the basement of his house to start his "comeback."

Keeping physically fit was one thing, but John also needed to keep mentally fit and stay productive. So he started graduate school at The University of Tennessee, he volunteered to be an assistant coach for the women's swim team, and he got a job bartending to make some spending money and meet people. He also knew that to catch the Navy's attention, and get back in its good graces, he would have to show that he was actively "staying Navy." So, for one weekend every month, John would drive nine-and-half hours from Knoxville to Virginia Beach, throw on his uniform, and "voluntarily" drill with the Navy SEAL reserves. He faithfully put his 13+ years of Navy experience to good use, working with fellow reserves, doing whatever was asked of him. John describes this time in his life as his "rebirth." The goal, again, was to demonstrate to the Navy what he had proven to himself: through and through, John Havlik was a Navy SEAL and belonged back on active duty!

There was something else John was doing for his comeback. A few times a week, in between school, swim practices
and bartending, he would go to the local libraries around
Knoxville, and spend countless hours reviewing his naval
records, agonizingly pouring over his files trying to figure out
why he didn't get promoted. John had a persistent nagging
feeling in his gut that a mistake had been made somewhere,
that something in the process just didn't seem right.

ONE CLUE CHANGES EVERYTHING

It was during one of those long monotonous library sessions,
tediously reviewing his records, that John noticed something
odd, something that had been there the whole time but hadn't
caught his attention before. It was on one of his past annual
fitness reports, the term the Navy uses for a performance
review document. The report that the Navy had as part of
its official records was *not the same* as the original report
John had signed and been provided a copy of for his personal
records. On this particular "official" fitness report was *a hand-
written change* (for the negative) in the "Recommendation for
Promotion" section.

Knowing this was potentially a big deal, John immediately contacted and later petitioned the Board for Correction
of Naval Records (BCNR) in Washington D.C., to have the
altered fitness report removed from his official records and
be replaced with the copy that John had originally signed,
because John had never been notified of that change, nor provided a copy of the changed report *as required by Navy policy*!

The BCNR eventually agreed with John's petition,
expunged the altered fitness report from his official naval

records, and replaced it with the copy of the signed original report John had provided in his petition. Additionally,
because a policy mistake had been made, John was told that
he had the right and grounds to appeal his two previous promotion non-selections to a special Navy promotion board,
because those previous promotion boards had not been given
information that reflected an accurate and complete review
of John's performance as an officer.

All the while, during the entire year-and-a-half process
it took to correct his record "mess," John was still diligently
working out, still coaching, still going to classes, still bartending, still working with the SEAL reserves, and most
enjoyably, beginning to plan his "second chance" return to
the active ranks of the Navy.

EARN IT

During his time out, John was also changing as a person. He
had grown more comfortable in his own skin, more confident
as a human being after hitting his humbling rock bottom.
Not arrogant in a chest-thumping bravado way, but confident
in who he really was as a person, and the foundation upon
which he was rebuilding his life.

The US Navy Special Warfare uniform breast insignia is
more commonly known as the "Trident", in recognition of
the weapon used by Poseidon, God of the sea. It is one of the
most recognizable breast insignia's in the Navy, and highly
coveted by SEALs, because of how difficult it is to earn! There
is also a saying in the SEALs that prior to being rejected by
the Navy had seemed like an abstract concept to John. Now,
though, that saying meant more to him than ever before, and

became part of his very core.....Earn your Trident every day!

Just about the time John decided not to appeal to a special promotion board, a different opportunity in the Navy presented itself. John *could return to active duty* if he joined the active reserves and, for his first assignment, be the Commanding Officer of a Navy reserve center. Like most good deals in life, there was a catch, in that he wouldn't be leading SEAL reservists on either coast like he had hoped. Instead, he'd be commanding Navy reserve personnel in the Great Plains state of North Dakota!

Yes indeed, *earn that Trident every day*!

John looks back at his two+ years in Fargo with fondness and a hint of amusement. "I was so happy to be back in the Navy that I didn't care about what they wanted me to initially do, but the cold weather up in North Dakota was absolutely brutal! The entire months of January and February the temperature rarely got above zero!" he says. But Fargo provided John with an opportunity to prove himself once again to the Navy brass.

One particular area that he focused on that he knew he needed to improve upon was becoming more "politically astute." If he wanted to take full advantage of this second chance in the Navy, he needed to learn how to play the game and get smart with the political realities of working within a political system. Though an introverted person by nature, John intentionally sought out and fostered relationships with a myriad of leaders in the local and state community while in North Dakota, including the governor, senators, legislators, and National Guard leadership, resulting in John being recognized as the 1999 Military Person of the Year by the Fargo/Moorhead

(MN) Metro Military Affairs Committee. Additionally, every six months, John would fly out to the SEAL training facility in Coronado, California, to maintain his diving qualifications (and thaw out), plus rebuild his relationships with the current leadership at the SEAL headquarters, and stay in the touch with what was happening in the community.

John was doing more than resurrecting his career; he was learning lessons that built his know-how and confidence. He learned that the cocky "kick ass" attitude that helps a SEAL perform in training or on the battlefield is not always the practical approach that makes you successful at leading everywhere else. John boils the key leadership lessons he learned to these three things:

1. **Learn to push away from your desk, walk the deck plates and talk with your people:** The people you lead need to know that you value them, their input and their knowledge. For some very practical reasons, as a leader, it's prudent to regularly interact with the lowest ranking members. First, it shows that you believe that they matter. Second, those folks will give you the ground truth about the condition of the command and its overall morale. Third, they're smart and they've got great ideas. People need to know that you are humble enough to admit you don't know everything, and that you want to learn from them, regardless of rank.

2. **Open Your Mental Aperture:** As a leader you've got to push against the natural inclination to think that you know what's best for all. Yes, as a leader,

you will grow in your know-how, influence, and experience over time. But you're also aging as you do, and you've got to actively seek out new ways of doing things so that you don't get complacent, stale or rigid in your ways.

3. **Have a "Check":** It's not enough to try and manage your own ego. You've got to rely on a few select people to manage it too. John learned to build a strong and trustful relationship with his senior enlisted personnel. He tasked them to call him out when he was becoming overbearing or letting his ego get too inflated. The stronger the relationship you have with your "checks," the more truthful they'll be with you. In a real way, they can help you keep hubris at bay. We'll revisit this tip, in greater depth, a few more times before this book is done!

John says that the biggest lesson he learned is that people will have a lot more confidence in you when you place your confidence in *them*. He says, "North Dakota reminded me of why I loved the Navy, where I got to meet and work with some dedicated and patriotic Americans! Many of my reservists were driving over eight hours one way, from remote locations across the state and very often in extremely dreadful weather conditions, just for the privilege to serve their country once a month. Their dedication to duty was admirable, and they proved invaluable to my rebirth as an officer."

TRUE CONFIDENCE DOESN'T SHOW OFF

Humility is important to leadership. But humility, for most leaders, is acquired (or lost) along the way. Leaders gain humility by suffering through hardship and setbacks, and like John, humiliating rejection. Yes, people want to work for confident leaders. But they also want to know that the leader's confidence is anchored to humility. They want to know that no matter how powerful a leader gets, he'll stay humble and will remember his roots. They want to know that the leader will honor the duty to serve and will never put his own needs above the needs of the people and mission he is charged with serving.

True confidence is full of genuine humility. True confidence doesn't need your affirmation. True confidence isn't threatened when others experience success or rise in the ranks. It takes joy in contributing to it. True confidence knows its own value, and is sober about its weaknesses. True confidence knows it can learn from everyone, and everyone deserves to be listened to and valued. True confidence doesn't need to pretend it's something it's not, or put on airs of superiority or invincibility. True confidence doesn't brag. True confidence is comfortable in its own skin, and wants to put you at ease so you can be comfortable in yours.

What John gained by working his way through his life "gut check" was true confidence. The kind of authentic confidence that's infused with a healthy dose of humility, and that an officer needs to effectively lead others. Over the course of his naval career, John had to re-earn his trident every day, but it eventually paid off. Drawing upon the hard and humbling lessons he learned during his bottom in Baltimore and Knoxville, and his rebirth in the tundra of North Dakota, John was able to honorably serve his country for another 17 years in the Navy, to include being selected as the 2001 Naval Reserve Association Outstanding Junior Officer of the Year (Full-Time Support), commanding several times, and completing numerous operational deployments in key senior leadership positions to named and classified operations around the world.

TRUE CONFIDENCE ISN'T
THREATENED WHEN OTHERS
EXPERIENCE SUCCESS
OR RISE IN THE RANKS.
IT TAKES JOY IN CONTRIBUTING TO IT.

QUESTIONS AND ACTIONS

In the next chapter you'll learn more about the importance of having "checks" on your ego. In the meantime, here are some questions and actions to help you get the most out of the chapter you just read.

- Have you ever experienced a "bottom"? What are some leadership lessons you had to learn the hard way? How do you carry the lessons you learned into how you lead today?

- When you think about your average work day as a leader, which do you do more: spend time with the people above you (for example in executive meetings), or spend time walking the deck plate (with people you outrank)?

- When it comes to true confidence (the kind that includes humility), how do you think your direct reports view you? How do you know?

- Who in your life serves as a "check" on your hubris? When was the last time someone called you out on your own BS or inflated ego? How did you react?

TIP COACH'S TIP
EARN YOUR TRIDENT!

List all the ways you believe that you "earn your trident every day" in your role as a leader. What else could you regularly do to earn it even more?

While I had to re-earn my trident (and my credibility) every day after I returned to the active Navy, the thing that I'm most satisfied with is that _I never quit_ when things got bad after I was initially forced out. Saying I was "bummed out" would be a gross understatement. The truth was that I was in a deep and dark place, but thanks to a small group of true friends/colleagues and a lot of hard work, I was able to persevere and achieve my goal of getting back in the Navy and being a SEAL again.

Bottom line: everybody gets thrown some lemons in their lives, so it's up to you how "sweet" or "sour" you make your lemonade!

CHAPTER 7

Living Leadership

BRACE YOURSELF FOR A TOUCHSTONE TRUTH

There's something you need to hear if you're to be entrusted with leading others. It's something that you've probably not read in another leadership book, but something you deserve to know. Keep this in the forefront of your mind as you meet the challenges, and reap the rewards, of leading others. We think this insight is the most important and valuable advice in this entire book. Use this touchstone truth to keep your ego in check, your aims directed on those you're leading, and your heart humble. But because of the potency and pungency of the message you're about to read, it will be hard for your eyes to read, your ears to hear, and your mind to wrap around.

We're going to share this knowledge with you to help you be a more grounded and effective leader. The words we'll use will hit you between the eyes, not to hurt your feelings or put you down, or be disrespectful or crass. They may not be the cuddliest of words, but they will certainly startle you back to reality. They are words we actually use with each other, when either of our egos needs pruning. Hang onto these words when you're feeling overly prideful about the results you're achieving and the impact you're having. Remember them constantly as you advance and become responsible for leading more and more people. You will need perspective, sobriety, and levelheadedness when the seductions of leadership intensify, when your power grows, and when the temptation for your hubris to swell is strong.

The message is simply this: regardless of how substantial the results you secure, or how high the rank you achieve, or how much wealth you attain, or how many lives you impact, or how much deference or applause you receive, in the grand scheme of life, *you ain't shit.*

Remember these humble punch words and you'll do very well. Why? Because you'll be in charge of your ego, instead of the other way around.

KEEP LEADERSHIP IN PERSPECTIVE

As you progress in your leadership career and grow in influence, rank, and stature, never lose sight of the fact that you're just a tiny speck in an infinite universe, like every other human being who ever lived...and died. It doesn't matter how much money you make, how many people you lead, or how many grand achievements you amass, you will meet the same fate as everyone else. No one, regardless of status, escapes the descending ceiling which closes upon each of us, mercilessly, with each passing day. The old Italian proverb sums it up well, "At the end of the game, the king and the pawn go back in the same box."

Faced with its own mortality, what's an ego to do? Well, what it's always done: protect you from harm and danger. Self-preservation is the ego's most basic function, even if it means defending you from inescapable realities like your fallibility and imperfections. In this way, your ego is both your greatest ally and worst enemy. It protects you through duplicity. Without self-discipline, humility, and outside "checks" – which you'll learn about in this chapter – your ego can come to inflate your sense of self to the point where all that matters is gratifying your own needs, prioritizing your own desires, and perpetuating your own leadership existence. The ego can puff up your self-importance until, eventually, you come to view those around you as lesser, irrelevant, and expendable. The bigger the ego gets, the more objectified and insignificant others will become, unless they have big egos too, in which case you'll view them as competitive threats who, driven by their own ego-infused insecurities, could puncture the thin membrane of your leadership facade.

YOU DECIDE WHETHER THE *KILLER* WINS

You may find it surprising, but what the *Killer* does with you and your leadership is up to *you*. Hubris wreaks havoc when your self-will runs amok. Hubris appears when you let your leadership power go to your head and you become enamored with your own specialness. The *Killer* arises from immodesty, immaturity, and, above all, ego mismanagement. Yet, all it takes to make the *Killer* irrelevant is to stay humbly grounded in the ordinariness of your humanity.

Keeping hubris subdued requires always remembering the severe damage your leadership will do if your ego grows too big. Every person, regardless of upbringing or education or economic status, has the potential to do harm when they're charged with leading others if their ego gets the best of them. For this reason, and to keep hubris perpetually at bay, never lose sight of your nonspecial, very commonplace, and ever-present *ain't-shitness* as you progress in your leadership. How often does a leader need to remember this essential hubris-neutralizing truth? *Every. Single. Day.*

It is interesting that the words "human" and "humility" have similar origins. Both stem from the Latin word *humus,* which means "earth" or "grounded." Other related Latin words include *humanus, humilitas,* and the adjective *humilis.* The "hum" part of *hum*an and *hum*ility are connected. Both, essentially, mean *earthly* or *earthy* (of the earth). To be human and to have humility, essentially, means being *down to Earth.*

We are wired to want to excel, achieve, and advance. But when our egos cause us to lose the essential connection to our terrestrial humanity, we become untethered from humility, transfixed on our own interests, often to the point of excluding or even harming the interests of others. The hunger to excel is good, provided it stays rooted in humility. Aspiring leaders should always heed the old Mexican advice: *Vuela tan alto como puedas sin olvidar de donde vienes.* Fly as high as you can without forgetting where you came from.

EVERY PERSON HAS THE POTENTIAL
TO DO HARM WHEN THEY'RE CHARGED
WITH LEADING OTHERS IF THEIR EGO
GETS THE BEST OF THEM.

REACH FOR *THRIVING LEADERSHIP*

So far, our focus has been on hubris and other related factors that will suck the life out of your leadership. But our ultimate aim is to help your leadership be full of life. Much of this chapter will focus on actions you can take not just to mitigate hubris, but to help your leadership flourish. Call it *Thriving Leadership.*

When leadership *thrives,* optimism captivates the leader and those being led, permeating the relationship between them. When leadership *thrives,* people welcome challenges as opportunities to step up to a higher game, develop new skills and competencies, and rally together. When leadership *thrives,* communication flows freely, transparently, and frequently, as people speak candidly, respectfully, and passionately. When leadership *thrives,* people have deep confidence in themselves, each other, and in the team's direction. When leadership *thrives,* everyone can be relied upon to respect and support each other, give their best, and get the job done. When leadership is truly *thriving,* the whole work atmosphere is positive, energetic, and uplifting. You know those days when you actually *want* to go to work? There's a good chance it's because leadership is *thriving.*

Just what does it take to have *Thriving Leadership*? Ego management!

LEADERS DO BEST WHEN HELPING OTHERS DO BETTER

Alex Okosi was getting set to become a student in an executive development program at the Harvard Kennedy School when we interviewed him for this book. Alex is an executive vice president and managing director of Viacom

International Media Network, and is responsible for Viacom brands throughout the African continent, as well as the BET Network internationally. We asked him whether he ever came face to face with his own ego and what the experience taught him. His story offers insights to those who pay attention.

Though born in Nigeria, Alex was educated in the United States. During his teens, he attended Greece Olympia High School in Rochester, NY, and became a star basketball player. During a particularly memorable game, Alex scored an amazing 38 points out of the team's overall 50 points. As his coach drove him home after the game, Alex was feeling cocky, having just proven himself to be the best player on the team. But instead of stroking his ego, his coach caught him totally off guard when he said, "If you're going to play like that, I don't want you on the team."

It's worth noting that Alex's coach was Jim Johnson, a celebrated high school coach who is now a nationally recognized motivational speaker. Okosi said the car ride conversation with Coach Johnson after his own game-winning shooting performance was one of the most important moments in his life. "The message was clear: being a great self-performer is not enough. Leading is not about you and how many points you score. If you're going to hog the ball and take all the shots, what do you need a team for? You may win that one game, but unless others also get to contribute and grow, the *team's* winning performance won't be sustainable. And your teammates won't want you on the team."

Alex says that he tries to carry the lesson he learned that day into how he leads now. He thinks of himself as a "player-coach" – someone who is vested in doing a great job for the business by doing right by his people. "If I stay focused on helping others be successful, I get better results and I enjoy myself more. Coach Johnson helped me switch the focus from myself to the people whose success is connected to my own. I'm a better leader when everyone plays at a higher level, and my job is to elevate people and their performance."

Ultimately, Coach Jim Johnson was doing for Alex what a good leader does: reach the better person behind the ego. He was helping Alex come to see a bigger picture that included the team's overall performance, not just his own. He was helping Alex learn the value of modesty and inclusion. In a subsequent interview with Coach Johnson, we asked him about his recollection of the car ride conversation. He confessed that, though he remembered Alex very fondly, he had no specific recollection about the conversation. "It sounds like something I would have said, though. It was easy to see that Alex had a tremendous amount of talent, and he was a great player. He just needed to learn what a lot of talented young players need to learn: how to bring people with you on a team. It's not enough to be a great player. You've got to be a great *team* player."

CHECK YOUR EGO

At this point, we hope you've become fully convinced of the dangers that your ego can bring to your leadership. Managing your own ego is vitally important to effective leadership. But it's hard to do by yourself. So we recommend having some "checks" on your ego. Meaning, you need to have someone who can act as a radar screen, and has your permission to sound the alarm when your ego starts to pulse too intensely.

Value this person, because as much as any other recommendation you'll learn from us, your "check" can help keep hubris at bay. A quick story illustrates the concept.

Kristie Kenney is a recipient of the Secretary of State's Distinguished Service Award and, in the course of her career, has held U.S. Ambassadorships in the Philippines, Thailand, and Ecuador. Being an ambassador carries a huge responsibility. As an ambassador in a foreign country, you are the President's highest-ranking representative and are responsible for carrying out the interests and policies of the United States. In addition to attending state dinners, negotiating treaties, and meeting with foreign dignitaries, you also coordinate the activities of upwards of 40 other U.S. government agencies so that everyone works in concert. It's not unusual for an embassy to have as many as 2000 working professionals, all of whom work under the ambassador's leadership.

Given the importance of the role and the power it carries, it's essential to have a few key staff members who can get through to you when your ego might be taking you in the wrong direction. When you are the ambassador, people are constantly deferring to you and agreeing with your sentiments, which, beyond a certain point, can become dangerous. You need a few select staff members who have your permission to "check" your ego, partly because of how ego-massaging it is to be in roles of stature like an ambassadorship, where you get constant affirmation of your specialness. As good as you may personally be at managing your own ego, it's critical to deputize a few key individuals who won't spoil or pamper you ("checks") and will give you strong doses of truth when your ego might be blinding you from it.

"During my first ambassadorship," Kenney said, "a senior member of the President's cabinet notified the embassy that he would be visiting the country. As the highest-ranking government diplomat in the country, I assumed that I would be invited to join his motorcade when he arrived. Like me, a lot of ambassadors refer to the country to which they're assigned as "my" country. I was eager to tour with the Cabinet member to introduce him to a place I had come to know so intimately and felt so attached to. But much to my disappointment, I was not invited to join the motorcade."

As Kenney explained it, she was a little miffed. After all, who would be in a better position to brief the cabinet member upon his arrival than her? Privately, she grumbled to her husband, who, himself a career diplomat, was very familiar with the standard protocols when dignitaries were visiting from the White House. "My advice?" her husband said, "Get over yourself. His trip isn't about you. Plus, you're an ambassador, not a member of the president's Cabinet. The quicker you stop bellyaching, the more you'll be able to prepare for his visit."

Kenney laughs about it now. "He was right, and it was the exact advice I would have given him. I was too caught up in my wah-wah, poor me, which was only getting in the way, and which my husband had no tolerance for." She goes on, "Once I got over myself, I was able to focus on what needed to be done to ensure a productive visit."

As Kenney explains, when you're in a leadership role, a lot of people will defer to you out of respect for your position. There are times, though, when that can insulate you from counter-opinions that might prevent you from making self-serving or bad calls. In addition to her husband, she also tasked her deputy ambassador (the Deputy Chief of Mission), and her executive assistants to keep her in check. She notes that it helps if they use humor, saying things like, "You seem a little short today, is there someone you'd like to vote off the island?" or "Is this something you'd like me to help resolve, or are you just spitting nails?" Occasionally, too, a check can hold you to a higher standard, saying, for example, "You let that person off too easy. I think you were overly benevolent. May I suggest you revisit that? You really should."

Put Humility to Work

Plenty of people think of themselves as humble, but don't behave that way. Arrogance shows itself in one's behaviors. So does humility. Here are some ways of actually behaving with humility.

ASK QUESTIONS: Leaders aren't expected to know everything about everyone's job. Otherwise, what would you need them for? But leaders *are* expected to be knowledgeable and informed. Don't be afraid to ask questions that might reveal your ignorance about a subject. Asking questions is the best way to show that you don't have all the answers, which others will appreciate.

SHOW YOUR WARTS: Don't pretend to be perfect, because you're not. People want to be led by leaders who are seasoned and scarred, because that's how wisdom is gained. Young professionals, especially, need to know about the mistakes you've made and the "do overs" you wish you could have. It helps them feel less awkward knowing that even leaders screw up.

SURROUND YOURSELF WITH PEOPLE WHO ARE SMARTER THAN YOU: The point isn't to outshine your direct reports. It's to help bring out the best in them in the service of the mission. Too many leaders default to hiring the least offensive job candidate. Instead, hire people who will lift everyone's game, including your own. Steve Jobs once said, "It doesn't make sense to hire smart people and then tell them what to do; we hire smart people so they can tell us what to do."

SPEND TIME WITH PEOPLE YOU OUTRANK: Drawing on his Navy SEAL days, John Havlik says, "You've got to walk the deck plates." The folks closest to the work need to know you're not out of touch with the realities and challenges of the work. Not only will they appreciate the access to you, they'll give you practical insights and ideas that will strengthen your leadership influence...and make you smarter.

OPEN YOURSELF UP TO FEEDBACK: How will you ever know if you're a good leader if you don't get feedback from the people you're leading? If your organization has a 360-degree feedback process, ask to go through it. If not, send an email to your boss, a few peers, and all your direct reports asking them three things: 1. What do they see as your leadership strengths? 2. What suggestions do they have for improving your leadership? 3. What resources can they recommend to leverage your strengths and help improve your leadership?

Leadership Caution: when you ask for honest feedback, be ready for both the good AND the bad! Don't be the hubristic leader who doesn't accept negative feedback, especially when you're the person who asked for it. Be like an Olympic diver: throw out the high and low scores, and take the average of the rest.

SAY "THANK YOU", SINCERELY AND OFTEN: It's arrogant to not acknowledge the good work of those who are actively contributing to your success. If you're one of those leaders who thinks, "Why should I thank them for what they're getting paid to do?" then you are *exactly* the person who needs to say "thank you" more often!

WHAT'S YOUR CHECK?

The actor Michael B. Jordon, star of *Creed, Fruitvale Station,* and *Black Panther,* talks about the importance of surrounding yourself with truth-tellers in a cover article in *Men's Health* magazine. In an industry literally built on applause, the temptation to get a big head is strong. Jordon's "check" comes in the form of a posse of friends who keep him real. "My boys are humblin'! If you heard a conversation from the

outside you'd be like, does this guy even like him? I have no
'yes men' around me...I don't believe my own hype."

How about you? Who has permission to help you check
yourself? Who is allowed to give you honest, unfiltered feedback without you feeling dissed? Who's allowed to clobber
your ego when it's getting unruly? Who is allowed to occasionally remind you of your *ain't-shitness*? Who is this trusted
confidant, this loyal ally, this true friend who looks out for
your best interests when your ego is working against itself?
Encourage them. Value them. Reward them. For they are
your best hope for keeping grounded and levelheaded when
your ego is gets overly inflated and aims to float into the
stratosphere. Your checks will do more than prevent hubris
from sabotaging your leadership. They will help your leadership *thrive*.

PICK A SIDE

We began by telling you that every leader needs to answer
this critical question: *How will I use my leadership power?*
We hope you'll consider all the ways that hubris damages the
leader and those being led. Where you direct your influence
and power is entirely up to you. You can use your power to get
more powerful, or you can use it to empower others. You can
focus on bettering peoples' lives, or you can exploit people
and lord over them to get your way. You can get busy serving
others, or you can fixate on having them serve you. What you
do with your leadership power really comes down to a simple
choice: will you *lead* or *rule*?

Be decisive but decide wisely. How you choose to use
your leadership power will determine your fate, wellbeing,

and legacy as a leader. Just remember that using power to feed, massage, and cater to your ego is the very essence of arrogance. Using power in order to serve and empower others is the essence of leadership.

So what will it be?

We trust you. You know the right answer.

In the Bonus Section, we'll share ten final tips to help you put your leadership power to good use, and to keep you from sabotaging your own leadership. Before moving on to that section, we encourage you to attend to these questions and tips.

- On a scale ranging from 1 to 10, with 1 being "too small", 5 being "just right", and 10 being "too big", what number signifies the size of your leadership ego today? Explain your pick.

- Have an honest conversation with your "checks" and let them know that you don't want to be surrounded by yes-people. Give them clear coaching on how to approach you when they have to deliver messages that your ears may not want to hear.

- List the people in your life that you've given candid feedback to along the way. Is there a difference between how you give candid feedback to a direct report, versus a peer or a boss? Based on the times you've delivered tough feedback to others, what tips would you offer a budding leader for when they have to deliver a tough message?

COACH'S TIP
FIND YOURSELF A SWIM BUDDY!

In SEAL training, we were assigned a "swim buddy" from Day 1 of training to the day we graduated. Once assigned, you quickly learned that you never went anywhere without your swim buddy, always within 6 feet of each other...or else you would suffer the wrath of the instructor staff! One Monday morning during training, we were in formation for the weekly haircut/uniform inspection. My swim buddy was running late as he put on his uniform in the locker room, and the class kept screaming for him to fall into formation as soon as possible, as the instructor staff was about a minute out from inspecting us. When he finally did fall in, much to the class's (and my) chagrin, my swim buddy's uniform, although clean and pressed, was heavily faded and his pants leg hems were about 8 inches higher than ours! As the phase officer stepped in front of us to inspect the formation, he immediately saw my swim buddy in the front row and his faded and ill-tailored uniform, and asked him to join him in front of the class. After berating my swim buddy for his substandard uniform appearance, the phase officer then ordered my swim buddy to "go get wet and sandy"! As my swim buddy started to run towards the ocean surf, the phase officer also said, "And take your dumbass swim buddy who let you wear that piece of crap uniform"...(or words to that effect that don't require editing). So, I too had to get wet and sandy with my swim buddy because I failed to "check him" before our inspection. The moral of the story is: whether you're putting on a uniform or making multimillion-dollar leadership decisions, you need to have a swim buddy to watch out for you.

BONUS SECTION

Ten Tips for Thriving Leadership

We hope that you've found these ideas useful and, in a healthy way, challenging. We hope that the exercises, advice, and Coach's Tips at the end of each chapter have been valuable for you. We offer the tips in this bonus section as a final boost to help you and your leadership impact thrive. They're focused on keeping you humble, balanced, and focused on those whom you're privileged to serve.

1. LEAD YOURSELF FIRST

Nobody wants to be led by a leader who can't even lead himself. Leading yourself is the starting standard that begins to qualify you to lead others. Here are some ways to tell if you're lacking in self-leadership:

- Your personal life is a mess.

- You're out of shape, physically, mentally, and spiritually.

- You're frequently in a state of anger and are quick to let your emotions get the best of you.

- You're disorganized, often miss deadlines, and frequently run late.

- You assume the worst first, and complain a lot.

- You mentally or verbally negatively judge others more than you should.

Self-leadership starts with a realistic assessment of your strengths and opportunities for development. It requires intentionally, consistently, and diligently improving yourself. Forever.

2. VALUE VALUES

The leaders we most admire embody and uphold enduring principles and values. They have a certain congruency – having values and living according to them. They are the opposite of hypocritical leaders that we don't admire – people who say one thing and do another. The difference between having values and living them, and saying you have them and not living them, is the difference between having and not having *integrity*. To be a good leader, you have to have good values. Take stock of what you stand for, and what you stand against. Consider:

- What values do you hold most dear?

- What values would others say you most embody?

- In what ways do your goals, priorities, and actions line up with your values? In what ways don't they line up with your values?

- Which values are nonnegotiable and define a boundary you will always uphold?

Value your values. They are the stuff that character is made of.

3. NAME YOUR FEAR

Hubris feeds on fear. The ego is designed to protect you from harm or danger, so it is hypervigilant against threats. The more threatened your ego feels, the more it will act preemptively against what it finds threatening. This protection mechanism is at the root of much of the intimidating behavior you see from arrogant leaders. At the core, arrogant leaders are fearful leaders. They externalize their own fear by intimidating you into being afraid of them. The more afraid of them you are, the less threatened they'll feel. Thus, to prevent yourself from becoming a fear-based leader, it's important to identify the things you find threatening. Here are a few common fears that arrogant leaders preemptively strike against. Which ones, if any, do you find threatening? Are there other threats you'd add to the list? What actions can you take to mitigate your fears so they don't get externalized in the form of intimidating behavior?

- Not being respected.
- Not getting what you want.
- Not being in control.
- Not getting results.
- Not getting fairly recognized and rewarded.
- Losing something you've earned.
- Being judged as less valuable then your peers.

When you feel fear, rather than letting it get displaced in the form of intimidating or abusive behavior, act with courage by exploring what's driving your fear, and working through it.

4. START AND END YOUR DAY WITH TWO KEY QUESTIONS

This tip is a few hundred years old, which speaks to its durability and usefulness. It comes from the autobiography of that truest of Americans, Benjamin Franklin. Each day, upon waking, old Ben would ask himself, "What good shall I do this day?" It gave his day immediate purpose, focus, and direction. This question helped orient all of his actions and conversations that day. It also helped him put on a service mindset. Notice the question isn't about productivity, it's about *goodness.* When most of us think about doing good we aren't thinking about ourselves. We do good *for others.* But the question itself requires a check. It's not enough to start the day with a noble intention. We must finish the day with careful reflection on the actual ways we have made a positive impact on the lives of others. After all, as a leader, what good are you if you aren't doing good? Hence Franklin's second question, which he asked himself each evening, "What good have I done today?"

5. RESPECT SELF AND OTHERS

Too many leaders pay lip service to the importance of respect, but are personally disrespectful. They show up late to meetings, they interrupt people, and they don't abide by the rules they want others to conform to. Relying on your rank or title is a cheap way to get respect. Real respect is *earned*, day in and day out. How? By doing such things as...

- Making others feel important by treating them like they matter, regardless of their rank, because, guess what?...they do!

- Seeking out and listening to the insights and ideas of others, and taking their concerns seriously. Remember, your success as a leader is dependent upon their good work. So they matter more to you than you do to them.

- Acting like an adult is supposed to act. Don't fly off the handle when people make mistakes, and when engaged in conflict, fight fair. Don't use fear to motivate people. Don't manipulate others just to get your way. In other words, keep your emotions in check. If you aren't able to, consider seeking help, because you might not actually be an adult, but some kind of baby that managed to rise through the management ranks!

- Apologizing quickly, candidly, and sincerely. When you mess-up, fess-up.

- Producing. Talk is cheap. Real leaders do real work and make real things happen. One of the leaders we worked with, the director of a scientific research center at a leading university, said it best, "Get shit done."

- Being self-respectful. Having and upholding boundaries and saying "no" when they're crossed. Trusting your instincts by listening to, and following, your intuition. Being good to your body and nourishing it with good food. Using positive internal "self-talk", and giving yourself credit when you do a good job.

6. PLAY THE TAPE FORWARD

The little word "lead" in the big word "leadership" means to *stay out in front*. As a practical reality, you aren't leading if you're only operating in the here and now or living on the glories of the past. As you lead today, you've got to do so with an eye toward a better tomorrow. You've got to assess each direct report not just according to the competencies and skills that they've got today, but the ones that they will require to meet the needs of tomorrow. You've got to forecast what your team, department, and/or organization needs to look like when it is operating on all cylinders. And you've got to be thinking about what a better, more informed, more experienced, and more humble *you* looks like a few years hence. Take everything you're contending with as a leader today, and play the tape forward toward the ends that you'd like to see. Then identify the specific actions that will increase the probability of those ends playing out.

7. BALANCE WHY, WHAT, AND HOW

As a leader you've got to constantly communicate three things:

- Why your team does the work it does.
- What everyone needs to do better.
- How everyone's work fits into something large and important, and how everyone is expected to interact with one another.

Leaders often overcommunicate the "what" and undercommunicate the "why" and "how," because "what" focuses on the stuff they really care about: goals, tasks, and results. Leaders commonly fear that results will suffer if they stop talking about *what* needs to get done. But people need to know *why* those results are important to the organization and its future, and *how* their work contributes to achieving those results. *How* also pertains to how people will be expected to conduct themselves in pursuit of the results. Being clear about *how* people should be expected to behave, carry themselves, and interact with one another is every bit as important as *what* they need to get done, and *why*. *How* defines the means to the ends (*what*) you're aiming to achieve, and *why* defines the reasons those means and ends matter.

Using percentages, identify the amount of time you currently spend communicating the *why*, *what*, and *how* of work to see if they're out of balance (it should add up to 100). Start ramping up the time you spend communicating whichever one you're currently neglecting.

Why:

What:

How:

While you're at it, how would you answer the *why*, *what*, and *how* of your leadership career? *Why* do you choose to lead? *What* do you aim to get done through your leadership? *How* will you behave, carry yourself, and interact with others as you lead?

8. POLISH YOUR CONSCIENCE

Live in a way that you'd never be embarrassed to read about any aspect of your life on the front page of USA Today. Do things that keep your conscience clear and clean. Read spiritual literature to keep yourself well attuned to the differences between right and wrong. Donate your time to a worthy non-profit organization where you can anonymously serve others who don't enjoy the same advantages as you. Never miss an opportunity to help others in need, stand up for those who might be challenged to stand up for themselves, and mentor those in need of direction. Do things that feed your soul and nourish the souls of others.

9. BE GRATEFUL AND GRACIOUS

In the grand scheme of things, you're here on this Earth for an infinitesimally short period of time. Life is precious and fleeting. Be thankful for all of those who are on this journey with you, regardless of whether they see the world as you do. Also be grateful for the people whose lives you get to impact through your leadership. Without them, you wouldn't even be a leader, right? The best way to develop an "attitude of gratitude" is to continuously take stock of all the reasons you have to give thanks, and all the people who are furthering your life.

Having gratitude is not enough. You've got to hand it off to others! Let people know why you're grateful for them and the impacts they've made on you and your life. Gratitude and humility go together. Don't be stingy–express your gratitude humbly and generously!

10. ONE MORE TIME: EARN YOUR TRIDENT EVERY DAY!

Leadership is hard. Get used to it. You're going to have to deal with challenging and changing situations, limited and ambiguous information, and fickle and idiosyncratic people. It means getting shaded by others when things go wrong, and letting others bask in the sunshine when things go right. It means doing your level best to satisfy the competing needs of others, and often ending up letting everyone down a little bit. *Earning your Trident every day* means accepting all the harsh realities that accompany being in a leadership role and making the best of it! The good news is, as hard as leadership is, it's also fantastically rewarding. Getting to contribute to the growth, development, and advancement of others is more than a great thrill. It's a profound privilege.

ACKNOWLEDGEMENTS

Bill Treasurer's Acknowledgements

I never planned on writing this book. It surfaced as an idea only after I reconnected with my coauthor, John Havlik. Among the alumni of the West Virginia University Swimming and Diving Teams, John is truly a legend. It's not just because he's a badass Navy SEAL, it's because his swimming talents earned him an induction into the university's Sports Hall Of Fame. I am humbled that he got interested in this project and fully committed himself to it. Our Sunday morning reviews strengthened the book, and gave me a unique insight into the heart of a Navy SEAL. John is a great patriot and a good man. I'm lucky he is my friend.

I am fortunate to have a career that revolves around leadership. I have been blessed to have learned from thousands of experienced and emerging leaders as they've struggled to make a positive difference in the world. It's because of them that I get to do what I do, and I am a better man because of what they've taught me.

A few clients deserve to be singled out for the in-depth work we've done together, co-creating unique leadership development programs. Foremost among them is Aldridge Electric Incorporated. We've launched some truly unique programs together, many of which have influenced the programs my company has developed for other clients. Other great clients include Walsh Construction, Plote

Construction, Total Petrochemicals, The Co-operators, and Sachse Construction.

I've got some rather strong views about the good and bad of leadership. Special credit goes to the friends and colleagues who have shaped my thinking, especially: Hines Brannan, Ken Aldridge, Dan and Matt Walsh, Steve Rivi, Tom McLinden, Dan Plote, Jim Kouzes, Elaine Biech, John Ryan, Fred Jewell, and all the alumni of the Aldridge Electric VP Executive Development Program, Walsh Group Leadership Initiative, and Plote Leadership Program. A debt of gratitude is also due all of the fantastic leaders and luminaries who wholeheartedly endorsed this book. Thank you for your wonderful encouragement!

If I were to plot the amount of time I've spent conferring with clients prior to each engagement, I'm sure I spent the most amount of time with these people: Craig Atkinson, Mike Calihan, Krista Roberts, and Jerry Reece. It's truly a pleasure working with each of you.

A lot of good folks have worked with Giant Leap Consulting over the years. Special recognition goes to Becky Jarrell, Ahli Moore, Laura Cohn, and Justine Foo. You all have done amazing work!

I think of Nancy Breuer as my "voice coach." She's great at helping my writing sound like the me I was supposed to sound like. She is the founder of Clear Magic, and she has now strengthened my writing voice on three of my books. Thanks, coach!

As a writer, consultant, and keynote speaker, it takes a lot to get noticed these days. I'm thankful for the good work of the social media teams at Bright Planning and Weaving Influence.

The good folks who read my books and come to my keynotes and workshops are the reason I even have a career. Thank you for all you've taught me, and for giving me purpose and direction. I promise I'll never take you for granted.

I spend too much time on the road. The best part of my week is coming home to a family that loves me. Shannon, Bina, Alex, and Ian make life worth living. I love you!

John Havlik's Acknowledgements

never planned on writing a book. In fact, writing of any kind has always been difficult for me, and like office "politics," I avoided all dealings with it as much as I could. But when Bill asked me if I would coauthor this book, I immediately said yes! What an opportunity, I told myself!

Since retiring, I've enjoyed speaking in support of Bill's "courageous leadership" workshops around the country, and have additionally enjoyed reading Bill's four previous books. When we would talk about the concept of hubris and how it makes good leaders go bad, we both agreed that the need for this book to be written and released as soon as possible was a no brainer. And now, after having coauthored it, I only wish that a book like this would've been available for me to read back in 1984 when I started my career as a naval officer!!!

I am humbled for the opportunity to share a few of my "sea stories" with the reader. My leadership pedigree includes eight years of world-class-level swimming and coaching, followed by 29 years as a Navy SEAL officer, which afforded me many opportunities to work with and be led by a lot of good (and bad) leaders. As an officer, I also had the great honor to lead and work with many extremely brave special operators, whose super Type A egos (and hubris) were often way out of control. From all of them, I took pieces of their best and worst traits, and mixed them all together over the years to make a magical potion that helped shape my leadership "style." Unlike many of the former military "superstars" currently glamorized in Hollywood and social media, I was far from perfect in my career, made some stupid mistakes (especially in my early SEAL years), but in the end, I'd like to think that I developed into a solid, reliable, fair and consistent officer, who could make a decision - the skills *I feel* are required to be a good and effective leader in any profession.

Bill previously addressed and thanked many of the folks required behind the scenes to publish this book. I won't do that again but will offer a collective "Thank You" to all who supported this project. There are a few folks who deserve to be singled out for their support to me over the years. Specifically:

- To Bill, for affording me the awesome opportunity to coauthor a book! Bill is a courageous leader, and despite being a former diver, an all-around good guy! I'm grateful we've re-connected our friendship after all these years.

- To my sister Beth, who allowed me to travel the world and fulfill my dream of being a Navy SEAL! "Thanks" is too easy! I know I don't say it enough, but I love you.

- To my many coaches, thanks for seeing something in me that others didn't and giving me the opportunity to swim fast!

- To my many teammates, both in the pool and in the SEALs, thanks for your tireless support, advice, and keeping me on my toes!

- To West Virginia University, I am, and will always be, proud to be a Mountaineer!

- To Instructor "Psycho," thanks for setting me straight during Hell Week when you told me to NOT make a decision in 30 seconds that I would have regretted the rest of my life!

ABOUT THE AUTHORS

BILL TREASURER is the chief encouragement officer of Giant Leap Consulting, a courage-building company that is on a mission to help people and organizations be more courageous so they can drive out fear and produce exceptional results.

Bill is the author of *A Leadership Kick in the Ass* (Berrett-Koehler, 2017), that highlights how critical it is that leaders make a "Holy Shift!" – shifting their attention from themselves to the people they're privileged to lead. Bill is also the author of *Leaders Open Doors* (ATD Press, 2014), which focuses on the key responsibility leaders have to be opportunity-creators. Bill donates 100% of the royalties from the book to programs that support children with special needs.

Bill is also the author of *Courage Goes to Work* (Berrett-Koehler, 2008), an internationally bestselling book about how to build workplace courage. Bill is also the creator of the world's only do-it-yourself courage-building training program, *Courageous Leadership: Using Courage to Transform the Workplace* (Wiley Publishing, 2011). The program promotes leadership courage and has been taught to thousands of executives throughout the world.

Bill's first book, *Right Risk* (Berrett-Koehler, 2003), is about smart risk-taking and draws on Bill's experiences as a professional athlete. Bill is a former captain of the U.S. High Diving Team and has performed over 1500 dives from heights that reached over 100 feet.

For over two decades, Bill has worked to help leaders be more courageous, just, and effective. You can read about his company's impressive client list in the "About Giant Leap Consulting" section below. Bill attended West Virginia University on a full athletic scholarship, and received his master's degree from the University of Wisconsin.

Connect with Bill through social media: Facebook (http://facebook.com/bill.treasurer), Twitter (@btreasurer), and LinkedIn (www.linkedin.com/in/courage). To inquire about having Bill conduct a keynote for your organization, email info@giantleapconsulting.com or call 800-867-7239. Learn more at BillTreasurer.com.

CAPT JOHN "COACH" HAVLIK, US Navy (Retired), retired from the Navy in 2014 after 31+ years of distinguished naval service, 29 of those years in the Naval Special Warfare (SEAL) community.

Coach graduated from West Virginia University with a B.S. in Business Administration (Accounting). He was a 4-year swimming letterman, and his career was highlighted by being the first swimmer in school history to qualify for the U.S. Olympic Swimming Trials (1980), qualifying for the NCAA Division 1A Swimming Championships (3 times), and serving as tri-captain of the first undefeated men's swim team in school history his senior year. He was inducted into the West Virginia University Sports Hall of Fame Class of 2017, and, in 2018, became the first former WVU male swimmer selected for the Mountaineer Legends Society, WVU's version of a sports Ring of Honor.

Coach enlisted in the Navy in 1982, and was assigned to the United States Naval Academy as a swim coach/physical education instructor. He was later commissioned as a naval officer via Officer Candidate School in November 1984. Coach successfully completed Basic Underwater Demolition/SEAL (BUD/S) training in 1985. His career military assignments included a full range of duties in Sea, Air, Land (SEAL) Teams, Special Boat Teams, and the elite Naval Special Warfare Development Group. He commanded several times during his career, and completed numerous deployments in key leadership positions, supporting various worldwide military operations, to include Operations Enduring Freedom, Iraqi Freedom, and New Dawn.

Coach completed graduate studies at the Naval War College in Newport, RI, receiving a M.A. in National Security and Strategic Studies. Currently residing in Tampa, FL, Coach is the CEO of JRH Consulting, offering individual/team consulting on building and leading high-performance teams. He is also the Special Advisor for Giant Leap Consulting, a courage-building company focused on helping people and organizations act with more courage.

To contact or learn more about John, visit his website: www.coachhavlik.com.; Twitter (@CoachHavlik).

ABOUT GIANT LEAP CONSULTING

GIANT LEAP CONSULTING (GLC) is a courage-building company that is on a mission to help people and organizations act with more courage. Since its founding in 2002, GLC has conducted over 1000 client engagements to help individuals and organizations perform at a higher level. Our services include:

- **Courageous Future:** Strategic planning to rally the organization around a bold and compelling vision for the future.

- **Courageous Leadership:** Comprehensive leadership development and succession planning programs for emerging and experience leaders.

- **Courageous Teaming:** Teambuilding programs to strengthen and align senior executive teams.

- **Courageous Coaching:** Individual coaching to strengthen the leadership skills of managers and executives.

- **Courageous Development:** Skill-building training workshops for all employees, covering such topics as Culture, Leading Change, Professionalism, Team Leadership, Decision-making and Risk-taking, Presentation Skills, Strategic Thinking, and many others. We specialize in custom-designed workshops.

Giant Leap is proud of its client list, which includes, among others, NASA, Lenovo, eBay, Saks Fifth Avenue, Walsh Construction, Aldridge Electric Inc., Spanx, Novo Nordisk, Plote Construction, the Pittsburgh Pirates, the CDC, and the U.S. Department of Veterans Affairs. Through our work with the National Science Foundation, we have facilitated strategic planning engagements at Harvard University, Massachusetts Institute of Technology (MIT), Yale University, the University of Massachusetts, University of California at Berkeley, University of Southern California (USC), Brown University, and many other renowned institutions of higher learning.

To learn more about Giant Leap Consulting,
visit our websites:

www.GiantLeapConsulting.com,
www.ManagerialCourage.com
www.CourageBuilding.com
www.LeadersOpenDoors.com.

To contact Bill or John about working with
your organization, send an email to info@
giantleapconsulting.com or call 800-867-7239.